Decent & Nadja Levs

Poverty and Alternative Economy

Root Causes of Poverty and
Holistic Solutions

**Extending Hope
Publishers**

POVERTY AND ALTERNATIVE ECONOMY - Root Causes of
Poverty and Holistic Solutions

ISBN 978-99908-0-242-9

Email: extendinghope@livenet.ch

Printed by lulu.de

Content

Acknowledgements

We want to thank Chris Child who helped to lay a good foundation in our lives and continues to influence us. His teaching and council helped us to develop a biblical perspective on life and contributed to fulfilling the vision of writing this book.

Many thanks also to Markus Reichenbach, leader of the School for Biblical Christian Worldview in YWAM, Wiler Switzerland who critiqued the content, Tabea Bärtschi who edited it, our Malawian friends who gave us ideas and stories for this book and many more people who encouraged us during the writing phase.

Introduction

Discover in Order to Recover

This book looks at the biblical view of poverty and highlights important principles for biblical economics through which people can experience the blessings of God described in the Bible. When we look at the world economy today, we see a growing global crisis that includes increasing levels of poverty and mismanagement of businesses and banking funds, both leading to struggles in world trade. Natural and structural catastrophes have also hurt the global economy. We wonder where our world is headed! From our discussions with students we got the impression that the universities of our time are properly training students to be good employees, but are not preparing them to be good employers. Many graduates today think they have to find a job within an existing company to earn their living. New graduates often lack the creativity to start something new. We want to challenge Christians, and all who read this book, to think outside of the box. We are living in a time in which many people are unemployed and it seems there are not enough jobs for everyone. We heard of occasions where there were more than one hundred applications for one job vacancy! That's why we have to be more creative in generating new job opportunities. For this reason, we compiled foundational principles from the Bible which are essential for the development of a long lasting and successful business and a strong global economy.

But in order to build a strong economy we first need to discover what has brought us to the situation we are in now, in order that we can recover. Our economy can be compared with somebody who is sick. That person goes to the Doctor to discover what the cause of the sickness is so that he or she can get the proper treatment. Thus we need to discover the root causes of our economic problems first, in order to find solutions.

We are challenging certain assumptions, beliefs and practices in the hope that the eyes of the reader will be opened to see the economy with a new understanding. Jesus observed in His time and said in Matthews 13:15 that people take things for granted without thinking critically and without understanding what to do to solve their problems:

> For this people's heart has grown dull, and with their ears they can barely hear, and their eyes they have closed, lest they should see with their eyes and hear with their ears and understand with their heart and turn, and I would heal them.' (Mat 13:15)

Our goal is to challenge you in the same way as Jesus did. We want to see the dull hearts and ears of people opened in order to apply the principles of God in economics. We want to see closed ears open to hear anew what God is saying in our crises today. We want to see closed eyes open to see opportunities and solutions for the present economy. The healing which Jesus spoke about would turn around our situation – the poor would improve their condition and the desperate would receive new hope. Jesus' mission on earth was to show us how we can live according to God's ways and enjoy the blessings of life with Him. That's why we are going to start with creation to discover the world of abundance (chapter 1) then we will discussion about the nature of poverty (chapter 2) and the causes of it (chapter 3). Building on the biblical understanding of poverty, we will look at possible solutions in chapter 4 and then emphasize the importance of strong families in chapter 5. Afterwards, we will discuss the five gates which influence economy (chapter 6), before we will look at practical principles of alternative economy (chapter 7) and finances (chapter 8) and discover what the Bible teaches on economic ethics, which are essential for a strong economy (chapter 9). Finally, in chapter 10 we will discuss the practical outworking of alternative economy by making suggestions on how to start a business, what to look for in the early stages of its growth (business cycle management) and how to plan its expenditures.

Chapter 1

World of Abundance

In our world there is a lot of potential which could help man to live a life in abundance. When we look at the story of creation in the beginning of the Bible, God did not intend the world to be full of poverty and brokenness as we are seeing it today. He created resources like rivers, lakes, land, mountains with minerals, sun light, and animals and these have been given into the hand of man to manage it and to turn it into wealth. Let us look closely at these resources and examine what we can do with them.

Land

Land is the most important factor in wealth creation. In the story of creation God planted a garden as a direct source of food for Adam and Eve[1]. They were told to manage it and to take care of it. Looking at the story of Abraham, his blessing was connected to a land. He was promised to be blessed and to be a blessing to many nations in the land which God was to show him[2]. Land can be used to cover basic needs as it

---

[1] Gen. 1-2

provides the place for a house or the ground to produce food. Thus the concept of agriculture was there in the very beginning of our history. Still today agriculture is one of the driving forces of economy: everybody needs to eat and food always comes from agriculture – no matter how developed a country can be.

Rivers and lakes

Water is another factor in wealth creation. It's again a resource which was given by God. It is very important – even for the survival of man, since man consists to 80% out of water. Water opens many possibilities. Rivers and lakes are filled with fish and there are oil sources on their ground. Their water can be used for irrigation in places or seasons when there is little rain. They can be used for shipping things and for the production of electricity

Mountains

There are different kinds of rocks and stones which can be turned into wealth. There are diamonds for jewelries, copper for cables, and hard rocks to build streets and foundations of houses. Further the mountains are a habitation for many animals which can be harnessed and turned into wealth - either by preserving them as tourist attraction, for food or as a helper of man.

Trees

Trees provide fruits for food and wood to fulfill various needs and purposes. Trees can be used for building houses, as energy source: to cook or to heat, as well as for medicinal purposes. They protect the land from erosion and communities from strong wind. They are even used to furnish houses with chairs,

---

[2] Gen. 12

tables, wardrobes, etc. In all these ways trees can be used to produce wealth.

Sun light

Sun light helps man to plan his time wisely, it shows the time and the season. Sun light provides heat and can be used to produce solar energy. Through this energy people can have light which allows them to work or study after sunset. It can also be used to cook in a solar oven or to dry agricultural products to preserve and use them at a later stage – for food or for cash.

Human power

> "I perceived that whatever God does endures forever;
> nothing can be added to it, nor anything taken from it.
> God has done it, so that people can fear before him"
> (Eccl. 3:14).

Man is the masterpiece of creation. When God created everything, he handed over the responsibility of stewardship to man. Man has got all the potential to unlock the world's wealth. God furnished us with the intelligence and creativity needed. We are called to be co-creators with God. We can use our human intellect to harness the resources given to us through human power. We can turn barren land into usable ground for agriculture production to produce abundance for our family and surplus for sells. There are still some scientists who say that man is an animal, therefore he should not exalt himself above the animal world. But one thing which we need to remember is that no other creature has got the responsibility which human beings have. Even if some say that man is destroying the earth and we need to take care of it. That's true, that's what God has planned. Why don't we go and tell the lions to preserve the earth? Because this task was given to man! It's only human beings who have the potential to care for the earth and to multiply its resources and to create wealth.

Looking at the resources explained above, we see that God prepared everything for man to live the life of abundance and not of need and brokenness.

We even see this in the promise God made to the Israelites, that there shall be no poor among them if they obey the voice of God in everything he commanded. This confirms what we know from the first chapter of the Bible, namely that God created everything good.

When we want to discover the causes of poverty in the next chapter, we have to keep in mind, that something went wrong with the world! Poverty is not just an economic issue or a lack of resources, but is a much more complex topic. After growing up in Africa where I experienced poverty, I came to Europe, and then had the opportunity to travel to Cambodia in Asia. By seeing the world from different continents, I started to understand that poverty is not just an economic issue. There are personal, political, social, religious and even supernatural dimensions attached to its causes. We will discuss what poverty is in the next chapter.

As a preparation to our studies of the nature of poverty, it may be helpful to think about the following questions. You could jot down some thoughts to every question before reading the second chapter about poverty.

1. Who are the poor (how do we know that somebody is poor?
2. Where do they live?
3. Why are they poor?
4. Where does poverty come from?
5. What will be the end of poverty?

Chapter 2

What is poverty?

When we talk about poverty, what do we mean? Who are the poor? If we look up the word 'poverty' in the Cambridge dictionary[3], it tells us that the meaning is "being extremely poor" and "having no basic living standard (food, clothing and a place to live)." But what is this basic living standard? How much food, clothing and housing must somebody have to escape this definition of poverty? Is somebody poor when he has a huge field, two sets of clothes and his own house, but only maize and sweet potatoes to eat? What about somebody who has no land, lives in a rented house and has to work in a company doing the same monotonous work every day, just managing to pay all his obligations at the end of the month, without time to relax and rest? What about somebody that has one million dollars but suffers from cancer and will die within two months – is this person rich or

---

[3] Cambridge Advanced Learner's Dictionary, 2005, p.985

poor? We see that the definition of poverty is not that simple at all.

Another common synonym of poverty is "neediness," "lack of something," or "a deficit in something". But who on earth lacks nothing? One may lack sugar, another lacks a good wife, the next lacks work, and another lacks rest. One has a deficit in speaking English; another does not know how to do agriculture. With this definition, everybody is poor! With this definition, we don't have a greater understanding of poverty. Let's see what the Bible says about poverty and its opposite - prosperity.

In Genesis, we encounter a young man called Joseph, who was a slave in the house of Potiphar, yet is called a prosperous man[4]. How can a slave without possessions and rights be called prosperous? Here, the actual meaning of prosperous is that Joseph was successful in everything he was doing. His work was of high quality, even when he didn't have any possessions. Later, this attitude of doing everything with a high standard manifested itself into material prosperity. Another scripture concerning the rich and the poor is in Revelation: Jesus calls the rich city Laodicea poor, wretched and pitiable[5]. This makes us wonder what the Bible teaches about poverty!

Let us now try to find out who are the poor people in the Bible. One interesting thing is that the Hebrew language has many more words than English. There are eight different Hebrew words in the Old Testament which are translated to "poor" in English. We are going to look at each one of them

---

[4] Gen. 39:2
[5] Rev. 3:17

to get a deeper understanding of who the poor are and what poverty means.

The eight Hebrew words for "poor" are the following:

1. 'ânîy (aw-nee'): depressed(afflicted)in mind or circumstances

This word is used when the Jews were commanded not to ask for interest on the money they lent to the poor (usury)[6]. It was also used when they were told to not shut their heart before the poor[7]. It is the same word which is used again and again by the prophets to urge the leaders to give justice to the poor. But David also used it when he said in the psalms that he himself was poor and needy[8]. Most of the time, this word refers to the poverty caused by injustice (meaning lack of social power), abuse of power, and lack of good laws that provide justice and security to everyone.

2. dal: dangling (weak, thin)

This word is used when God calls Gideon a mighty man, even though his family is the poorest one of their tribe[9]. They are weak and not suitable as soldiers in the army. In 2 Kings 24:14, we read that all of Jerusalem was carried away into captivity, except the poorest people. These were the people too weak to rebel. These were the sick and the old. In 1 Sam. 2:8, we read that God lifts this kind of poor out of the dust and sets them on thrones as princes.

3. 'ebyôn: sense of want (especially in feeling)

This is the word used when God told the Israelites that there will be no poor among them if they obey the commandments he

---

[6] Ex.22:25
[7] Deut. 15:11
[8] Ps. 70:5
[9] Jdg. 6:15

15

gave them. It is also sometimes translated as 'beggar' in English[10]
. It therefore suggests that it is poverty guided by feelings. A
person has to feel poor first, before he or she can go begging.

4. mûk (mook): to become thin, (figuratively) be impoverished

This word is used in the law where it speaks about
lending to someone in the community or about becoming a
temporary slave until debts are paid off[11]. This is a temporary
kind of poverty due to a sudden catastrophe in life. It can be a
business that went bankrupt or a natural disaster which left the
person without anything. In this case, the person needs the
help of the community so he or she can stand up again and
continue caring for himself and his family.

5. yârash yârêsh (yaw-rash', yaw-raysh'): being driven out and your property given to somebody else

One example of the occurrence of this word in the Bible is 1
Sam. 2:7 where it is said that the Lord makes poor and rich. This
kind of poverty is self-caused, due to lack of stewardship and
lack of obedience to God. This was the reason that God
allowed and even commanded the Israelites to take over the land
of the Canaanites, because their sin was fulfilled. We can also
compare it with the words of Jesus in the New Testament
concerning the parable of the talents: The one who buried his
talent had to surrender it to the one who multiplied his well.

6. rush(roosh): to be destitute

This word is used by David in 1 Sam. 18:23 where he calls
himself a poor man and in 2 Sam. 12:1 in the parable where
Nathan spoke to David about the poor man who only had one
lamb. It means to be very poor, especially in comparison to
the living standard of others. The poor man with one sheep
was compared to the one who had a whole flock.

---

[10] 1 Sam. 2:8
[11] Lev. 25:25, 35, 39, 47 & Lev. 27:8

7. chêl^ekâ' (khay-lek-aw'): to be dark, (figuratively) unhappy; a wretch

This word for the poor occurs only three times in the Bible. One example is a person who gets suppressed by the wicked and cannot do anything against it, because he is living in their midst in Ps. 10:10. In another place[12], the fatherless are called this way.

8. 'miskên (mis-kane'): indigent/a needy one

This word for poor is very interesting because all three times it is used in the Bible, it is related to wisdom. "But there was found in it a poor, wise man, and he by his wisdom delivered the city. Yet no one remembered that poor man"[13]. Although the poor are despised by the rich, they are wiser than the rich. This might also be said about serious Christians who do not have the same possessions as other non-Christians, but are much better off before God.

In the light of these different Hebrew words and the sample scriptures described in above and knowing about the complexity of the subject, we try to define poverty holistically as "being in mental, social, physical or spiritual affliction".

---

[12] Ps. 10:14
[13] Eccl. 9:15

Chapter 3

Causes of poverty

There are many different Hebrew words for poverty and even more different causes of it. In the following, we attempt to classify possible causes. We cannot discuss all causes of poverty in this book; the topic is too complex. We broke them up into four categories of causes: Natural and supernatural dimensions, structural evil, personal evil and inadequate worldview which will be explained in the following. After that we will address the root cause of all these.

Natural and Supernatural Dimensions
With natural and supernatural dimensions, we address those causes of poverty which are not directly within man's control. They are in connection to things that are wrong with our planet Earth or are coming from spiritual forces (good or bad). Natural disaster, sicknesses and diseases, famine, bad weather and lack of natural resources comes from both natural and supernatural causes. These are causes of poverty

which some people say are hard to influence, because they are not directly connected to human beings.

Structural Evil

Under structural evil are all the causes of poverty that come from human systems where people exercise abusive power and use others as slaves. It also includes different social conventions that promote poverty, such as corruption, oppression, exploitation, unjust resource distribution, favoritism, war and instability, bad leadership, abuse of power (in government & churches), bad stewardship (money, environment...), bad laws or bad implementation of laws, unjust banking system, unjust taxation and colonialism.

Personal Evil

There are also causes of poverty which are directly connected to bad actions of an individual. For these causes you cannot blame politics, the social environment or the supernatural. It is self- caused. The causes which fit into this category are broken relationships (marriage, family, business partnerships...), self- centeredness, selfishness, addictions (drunkenness), laziness (work or education) and poor planning. As a result of these bad actions, bad choices and bad habits, a person, whole families and communities can be trapped in chronicle poverty.

Inadequacy in Worldview

A worldview is a set of ideas and beliefs through which an individual interprets the world and interacts with it. As there are true beliefs and wrong beliefs, one can interpret the world rightly or wrongly and as a result, interact with it in a good or bad way. It is crucial to have the right biblical Christian worldview in order to be effective on earth. Having a wrong or inadequate worldview can lead to poverty. Examples of things that cause this category of poverty are superstition, having a poverty mentality, and fear of ancestral spirits.

Broken Relationships as Root Cause

When we dig deeper into the causes of poverty, we discover that the root cause is that we live in a fallen world. Sin entered humankind and affected everything. Now our relationships towards God, our self, people and our environment are broken. First, our relationship with God is broken, which leads to a wrong understanding of who God is. Because of this, we sin against him, which provokes supernatural judgment, which manifests itself in the natural realm as lack of rain and other catastrophes. Instead of doing what God intended us to do, we do what is right in our own eyes. This leads to personal evil. Even our view of the self is distorted (marred identity). We don't know who we really are and what we can do as human beings, created in the image of God. Instead of exercising dominion, we have a victim mentality that does not allow us to change our situation. At the same time, our relationships with our community and other people are broken as well. This leads to sinful behavior towards our neighbors. We steal, lie, cheat and murder. Because of these things, we make the lives of our fellows more difficult, unsafe and poor. It also leads to the social causes explained above as structural evil. Furthermore, we have to understand, that the poor don't live in a specific place among themselves, but among the non-poor. These are the people who have the material possessions or other assets which the poor in their community need. But due to broken relationships between them, the poor suffer and sometimes even get exploited by the richer people. It also happens the other way around; the poor people exploit and steal from the rich, so that they should become poor as well. The end result of this is that the whole nation becomes trapped in poverty. Finally, even our relationship with the environment is broken, which leads to the natural evil explained above. This broken relationship is responsible for the overuse of land, which even causes the land to become poor.

Chapter 4

Possible Solutions to Overcome Poverty

After seeing different causes of poverty in the previous chapter, we want to look at different ways poverty can be overcome. Any possible solution to overcome poverty needs to consider all the addressed causes of poverty. Any solution which only addresses one cause of poverty is doomed to fail, because it fails to be holistic. There are causes which we can directly influence (inside factors) and others which are harder to change by ourselves (outside factors). We must first begin with ourselves (personal evil & worldview) and then address the outside factors (structural evil and natural and supernatural dimension) by being planted in the system. To be planted in the system means to be an ambassador of Christ in the area of profession where God has called and gifted you. If you are called to be a politician you are to engage yourself in the building of God's kingdom in this domain and thus serve God at your working place. In that way, you can deal with the structural evil also, but only after you change yourself first. Once the whole nation turns back to the biblical principles, the natural and supernatural dimension of poverty will be dissolved by God himself (see blessings for obedience towards God's instruction in Deut. 28). If we take this view point we will not be helpless in view of natural disasters, because we are co-workers and creators with God. We would be like Abraham who argued with God about the destruction of Sodom and Gomorrah, of which God would have relented, if there were only ten righteous people living there. Of course we will not have utopia, disaster could still happen, but it will not be of the same magnitude as we experience it now.

To start with ourselves, we first have to restore our relationship with God to overcome personal evil and then analyze our worldview and align it with the word of God so that we can have a biblical view of reality.

Change of Worldview

Behold, I am doing a new thing; now it springs forth, do you not perceive it? I will make a way in the wilderness and rivers in the desert.
(Is. 43:19)

In the Bible we find many examples of how a worldview (ideas or beliefs) influence a person in the direction of either prosperity or poverty. One example is Isaac in Genesis 26: There was a famine in the land and people fled to Egypt. Isaac wanted to do the same, but God spoke to him to stay in the land and hold onto the promise of blessing which he gave to his father, Abraham. Therefore, Isaac cultivated the land and harvested one hundred fold. The Bible also shows us that the principle behind his success was the use of an irrigation system (water wells). The Philistines contrarily filled the wells with earth because of a wrong worldview (v. 15).

Now you can understand why the people had to flee. They thought their circumstance was terrible and unchangeable. Nobody was encouraged to dig wells, which would have solved their problem. But the God of the Bible can turn a desert into a fertile land. That's why even today the people in Israel are successful in their agriculture. It's all a result of the right or wrong worldview. While the Israelites produce so much that they even export their sweet potatoes and other products to Europe, the Palestinians are dependent on development aid and food supplies from Europe.

We have seen that our belief in God influences our life. But how does it work?
Our view of God shapes our belief system or worldview and then affects the way we act. Because Isaac had the right view of God, *"God is faithful to his promise,"* he had a good worldview, *"I can cultivate successfully despite the famine,"* and make good use of what I have *"I use irrigation to let my crops grow."*

To illustrate this principle, we are going to look at different religious worldviews. We start with Hinduism in India, a country with many people in deep poverty. Then we will discuss Buddhism, a religion which is growing worldwide and has a good reputation even in the West, while Buddhist countries are still struggling to get out of poverty (e.g. Cambodia). Then we will look at Islam, as well as the impact of Animism in many African countries and finally discover some wrong beliefs of Christians.

Hinduism

The symbol of Hinduism is a circle, because all life is one. The goal is to reach the center, which is the sign of oneness. While the outer part of the wheel always moves, the center does not. Thus, the goal is to stop moving, to stop acting, and to just accept or ignore the things which move and change in the world. Hindus believe everything is one. Everything is god. They worship the mountains, the rivers, the animals and also the higher caste people. Because they worship the river as a god, they cannot build a dam while the water floods their fields and villages. They cannot discover copper or iron in the mountain, because it is a god as well. Whatever happens to them is sacred. If you are from the low caste people, it is a sin for you to build a brick house, because you are appointed to be in the lowest part of society, due to your sins committed in your past life. Diversity is not allowed, because all should be one. Therefore, there is no creativity or personal growth. The most important thing for them is spending time in meditation to become one again with all creation. In this worldview, there is no foundation upon which to build strategies to eradicate poverty, because all is believed to be right the way it is.

Contrary to the belief that everything is god, the Bible forbids us to worship any other god apart from Him (Deut. 5:7). This shows that creation is not sacred and therefore is not to be worshiped. If you worship it, you make God, the creator of it, jealous and harm yourself. Instead of using the resources which God has given you, you begin to worship them. If you only worship God, you can use the copper from the mountain and build dams to keep the river from flooding. By doing so, you develop your country.

Buddhism

For our development practicum, we went to Cambodia for two months, where Buddhism is the most popular religion. As soon as we arrived, we noticed the many temples and shrines. Even people living in poor housing don't fail to have a nice Buddha altar to offer daily food sacrifices. We felt like Paul in Athens[14].

Buddha's teachings can be summed up in a transitional and illusionary understanding of reality. Nothing is permanent, except suffering. This universal suffering is produced by cravings and lust, both good and bad. The solution to break free from suffering and the endless circle of rebirth is to get rid of these cravings and feelings through meditation. Even if the monks have books in their monasteries, they don't read them, but only turn their shelves to meditate on the sound it produces. In this view of reality, there is no economic development.

Islam

The word *Islam* means "accept", "surrender", "submit". The first duty of a devout Muslim is complete submission or surrender to Allah. Islam was founded by Muhammad ibn Abdullah, the final prophet who was born in Mecca, Arabia in AD 570. He died 62 years later in Medina. Muhammad received revelations from an angel called Gabriel which were collected after his death and are today known as the Qur'an. The Islamic belief is fatalistic. Anything that Allah wants will happen. For example: There was a Muslim village in Mozambique in which the people believed that Allah had cursed the ground. Because of that they never tried to cultivate anything, but they travelled far away to another region to

---

[14] Acts 17

cultivate. Every planting and harvest season part of the family had to live in an improvised hut there, till they could bring the harvest home with a rented truck.

Another stronghold of Islam is that Allah is the master to whom human beings have to surrender. Thus they are like slaves. This reflects itself in the Muslim families: Because the husband is the master of his family, his wife is a slave, too.

For the radical Muslims who are following the revelations of Muhammad when he was in Medina, it is important to fight everyone who is not in submission to Allah, until the whole world is subject to him. This is called jihad. There is no time to waste for development! There will only be perfect peace once everyone is in submission to Allah!

Since Muhammad taught lying as a strategy to achieve military and political goals. Thus any agreements with Muslim countries will only stand as long as it profits the Muslim leaders.

Ways to develop or change the economic or political system can be discussed with radical Muslim leaders, but eventually don't lead anywhere. If there is a disagreement among parties, the answer is fighting.

Not so with the God of the Bible. With Him, there is a relationship and accountability. He is not self-centered; within the Trinity everything is discussed and the different persons submit to each other in love. We see that already in the first pages of the Bible where God spoke: "Let us make men" (Gen. 1:26). God did not create as an individual, but in a relationship (notice the word *us*). If people relate to each other in love on the same level as the Triune God of the Bible demonstrates, there will be a significant contrast to the described master-slave relationship which produces slavery.

Animism

"You shall have no other gods before me." (Deut. 5:7)

Animism is the belief in many spirits which influence the physical reality. The goal of life is to appease the ancestor spirits. If there is any problem in the natural world, it is believed to be caused by the ancestor spirits who have been offended and angered by something the people have done. In Malawi, for example, some people used to worship the spirit of Mbona. Whenever there was a drought, people danced to this spirit so that he could send rain. Or there is the spirit of Mvimbuza, who causes sicknesses. The solution is to dance to this spirit so that he leaves the person. There are many more practices in this category such as 'sadaka' (a practice in which the family of a dead person prepares a big feast for the whole community because they experience some dreams in which the dead person comes to beg them for food) – always with the goal to appease the spirits through sacrifices.

This kind of worldview leads to poverty. In 'sadaka' practice, for example, all the food which could carry the family over three months is used in one day to feed the whole community with the goal of appeasing the ancestor spirits.

Another problem is that the country cannot develop because the people are afraid of making the spirits angry. In animism, witchcraft is a stronghold and many people live in fear of it. If anyone moves forward, others become jealous and use witchcraft to bring the person down again. We see that such thinking and behavior hinders development.

To illustrate the destructiveness of this worldview, we have included below a true testimony that occurred in my home village in Ntcheu:

> We helped our parents build a house. After the basic structure of the house was finished, they started living in it. At that point, my

mother became sick. The sickness got worse and it was at this time that a certain gentleman told my mother she would die and the new house was the cause of her problem. From then on, our parents lived in fear of this spirit of witchcraft and what it could do to them. At times, we sent some money to help them finish the house on the outside, but they used it for other things. Why? Because they feared that if they made further improvements in the house it would make the sickness even worse.

This is why some people prefer to live in grass houses, which could break every year when the rain comes, so that no one will be jealous and use witchcraft against them.

But the God of the Bible prohibits practices such as child sacrifices, divination (witchcraft), interpretation of omens, sorcery (witch or witchdoctor), the use charms or mediums, and inquiring from the dead. These practices were the reason that God drove the Canaanites out of their land and gave it to the Israelites[15]. It is no wonder that even people who practice these things today cannot succeed.

Inadequate Gospel

Sometimes it's amazing to hear what some Christians believe about God, man, and different spheres of society such as the economy. Some believe that their task on earth is to merely save lost souls by evangelizing them so that Jesus – who is coming soon – will take them with their converts to heaven. There is no idea of long term discipleship or thought of how to live as Christians in the world until Jesus returns. In the previous century, the church did well in spreading the message of salvation, but not so well in gathering disciples. People put the Gospel of salvation into the larger category of the Gospel of the Kingdom. This also results in the wrong

---

[15] Deut.18:9ff.

understanding of the future of our planet, which is often thought to end in fire and destruction. This comes from a wrong interpretation of some scriptures in the Bible, but this book is not the place to explore that particular topic in greater depth. However, we do want to ask the following questions: "Is it biblical to think only about the destruction of the earth?" "If man is going to be taken to enjoy the heavenly bliss, where can we get hope for this world?" "Does it mean that the plan of God for the earth was shattered when sin came in?" If we adopt this kind of worldview it takes away any hope for our life in the here and now. If Jesus can come tomorrow, what motivation is there to start a business or company today? If this was true, by the time your business really gets going, Jesus might have come again and everything would be destroyed by fire.

A year ago, I was advised by a pastor not to continue with my studies. His concern was that by the time I would finish my studies, Jesus might already have come and everything would have been in vain. So he told me to focus on reaching the lost souls.

Jesus, however, taught his disciples to do business until he returns. We find hints of this in the parables of Jesus in the Gospel of Matthew. From 24:45 to 25:30 Jesus tells a series of three parables about his second coming. First, he warns us not to start behaving badly and say "the master is delaying". Then, he tells them the parable of the ten virgins, which again illustrates that we should be always prepared, even if it takes a long time till Jesus returns. Then, the parable of the talents is explained. Here, Jesus encourages us to multiply the things which he entrusted to us until he returns. That's why Martin Luther, the famous German reformer and founder of the protestant movement, said: "Even if Jesus comes tomorrow, I will still plant a tree today." Because nobody knows the exact time when Jesus returns, we have to make long term plans and investments, but at the same time be ready for his coming.

Learning from Israel

The history of Israel as a nation goes back to the time that they were slaves in Egypt. During those 400 years of captivity, they cried to God until he sent Moses to deliver them. After they finally left Egypt, they were a people without a written history that explained their roots. They were without any land, only having the promise of one. They did not have a government, and no one had experience leading, as they were all slaves at the command of the Egyptians. There was no education system, no economy and no military. This was the state of these 3 Million people when Moses led them out. How do you start making a nation out of them?

We have to keep in mind that their worldview was strongly shaped by the Egyptians, as they had lived there all their lives. Their thinking was shaped by the fact that they were slaves and could not accomplish anything. Moreover, they were used to the Egyptian practice of worshiping many gods and a pyramidal power structure. When Pharaoh had a problem with someone, he would kill them. A human being did not have much value. In the same way, Moses killed the Egyptian who was beating an Israelite, as it was the common way of dealing with the problem. In their worldview, it was normal.

We can also imagine that they struggled with the question of God's almighty power, particularly as they were faced with such terrible circumstances. This is one important reason why God had to deliver them with his outstretched arm. He did this with many signs and wonders, and by bringing judgment on the gods of the Egyptians. He turned the water of the Nile into blood, showing that he is more powerful than the Nile god. He darkened the sun, proving that he is above the sun god, and finally drowned Pharaoh, who was called the living god of the Egyptians, in the Red Sea. The first of the Ten Commandments refers to the manifestation of God's power by reminding the Israelites that it was their God who led them out of Egypt and therefore, they should not worship any other god. But we will come back to the Ten Commandments later.

Then, God gave Moses the knowledge and strategy needed to bind the Israelites together. First, they needed to have a story which explained who God is, who they are, what truth is, what went wrong in the world, and what their responsibilities are. All these answers we find in the five books of Moses, starting with the explanation of how this world was created, including how humans came into being, showing God as the almighty, good and wise Creator. This was followed by the information that man is created in the image of God, and thus valuable. Then, man was commanded to till and keep the Earth and multiply on it. Israel clearly saw that everything God created is very good, but at the same time, they understood why evil is present in the world. Man sinned against God, corrupting the world, and all life within it. Sin was also the reason they were in slavery. Jealousy infiltrated the relationships between the sons of Jacob, until they sold their brother as a slave, which later led to the slavery of all their descendants in Egypt.

After giving them the story and the explanation of who God is, who man is and what went wrong, they received the commandments so they could understand what the truth is and distinguish between right and wrong. They needed this foundation in order to live together effectively as a nation. It also shaped and transformed their worldview into a new understanding of reality.

Even in our study about biblical economy and understanding poverty, we cannot bypass the Ten Commandments. There has been no other nation on Earth that is, or was in, such a desperate situation as the Israelites when they left Egypt. Then, they were established as a nation which, still today, has a worldwide influence. We will come back to this after first looking more closely at the Ten Commandments.

The Ten Commandments

"The Ten Commandments...are not a set of harsh prohibitions imposed by an arbitrary tribal deity. Instead, they are liberating rules that enable a people to diminish the tyranny of sin; that teach a people how to live with one another and in relation with God, how to restrain violence and fraud, how to know justice and to raise themselves above the level of predatory animals."
(Russel Kirk)

We have discussed the historical background of the law and learned that it was given to Israel as a foundation for the building of the nation. So why should we still study this law today? Many people ask this question, as this law was given specifically to the Jews. The law was not written by Moses, but by the finger of God[16]. It is eternal[17] and universally

---

[16] Ex. 31:18

true. Jesus made it clear in the New Testament that he didn't come to abolish, but to fulfill the law[18]. And Jesus continues saying, we should keep and teach the law so that we will be called great in the kingdom of God[19]. That's why Paul confirmed that, as Christians, we uphold the law[20] because it is holy, righteous and good[21].

The law is still important for us, because it reveals the will of God and his character. It teaches us what is right and wrong or good and evil. In that way, it is a standard to which we can all refer to help us make right judgment in everyday life. The law judges us and condemns those who transgress against it. Finally, it points us to Jesus, as it shows us the need for salvation, and therefore the need for the Savior. The law tells you to be saved, but it doesn't save you. If you have been saved through the grace of God, does the law still have a function?

Yes, it still reveals God. It still tells us what is good. The difference is that one does not obey in order to be saved, but asks as a child of God: "How does my father want me to live?"

As saved Christians, we have to keep in mind that the standard didn't change! God cannot forget sin because it truly hurts him, it is destructive and it has to be punished – Jesus bore the punishment. What has changed is that the power to fulfill the law is given to us through the Holy Spirit. **The law still has function: The law is a revelation**

---

[17] Mat. 5:18
[18] Mat. 5:17
[19] Mat. 5:19
[20] Rom. 3:31
[21] Rom. 7:12

of the will of God and the character of God. It reveals what is right and wrong. After being born again, we still need the standard of the law to build a strong and prosperous society, and to have a mirror which shows us who we are in the eyes of God.

Let's have a closer look at the 10 Commandments and what they reveal about the character of God:

1

Israel, your God is the one God, Maker of heaven and earth, omnipotent, omniscient, omnipresent, the just one, the gracious one, He is worthy
and deserving of all worship and all obedience ...
... you shall have no other Gods before him

2

He is true, He is truth, His truth matches with reality, He is who He is and any other belief must be lying and will fail you, He is jealous for truth, He is jealous for you ...
... you shall not make yourself an idol

3

He is holy, He is good, His being is the foundation of the universe, His character and name is the foundation of all moral law, His character is the only possible set of values that is not self-contradictory, and the only set that produces life...
... you shall not make wrongful use of the name of the LORD your
God

4

He is the God of glory, the God of dignifying work, and of rest, the God of celebration, of right priorities, desirous of you and your time...
... remember the Sabbath day, and keep it holy

5

He is the God of origins, of fatherly love, of motherly nurture, of family, of good roots, of deep anchoring, of a sense of belonging and of safety...

... honour your father and your mother

6

He is the God of creation, the Creator of all existence; the only Source of life, all existence is through Him, in Him immense value is bestowed on human life, all life, strong and weak, perfect and imperfect...

... you shall not murder.

7

He is the God of relationship, the God of selflessness, the God of faithfulness, the All-powerful One who obeys His own word, the God who keeps His word, the vulnerable God, the covenant-keeping God...

... you shall not commit adultery.

8

He is the glad Creator of a material universe, the God of bounty, the generous God, the lavish God, the caring God, the Giver of growth, the sustaining God, the Provider-God, the Lord of plenty...

... you shall not steal

9

He is the trustworthy God, the reliable God, the law-abiding God, the God whose word stands in all eternity, the true God, the truth speaking God, committed to justice and reality...

... you shall not bear false witness

10
He is the thankful God, the giving God, the glad Giver,
the big-minded God, the sacrificial God, the releasing
God, rejoicing with others, the God of joy...
... you shall not covet

(SBCW, 2009)

When God gave the Ten Commandments to the Israelites, He laid the necessary foundation for another worldview – an interpretation of the world which defined God as one, an almighty and just God who is concerned with righteousness and justice and man as made in the image of Him. By having these Ten Commandments, they were given a common reference point to worship one true God. This gave the foundation for one common worldview, one different from the Egyptians who entertained many different worldviews, depending on the character of the god they worshipped. Moreover, the commandments spoke into all areas of life. Commandments One through Three teach us who God is and our attitude towards him. Commandment Four bridges the gap between the first three commandments and deals with our attitude toward God. The last six speak about our attitude towards other people. They regulate the **work** of man and grant him **rest** from his work, in the form of worshipping God. Commandment Five values parents as the founders and leaders of the **family**, the smallest unit of a society. Commandment Six sets a standard for the national **government** and judicial system to protect human life and punish those who take it away. Commandment Seven speaks again about **family** and shows the importance of faithfulness in this fundamental unit of society. Commandment Eight protects **economy** by ensuring that everyone should eat the fruit of his work. Commandment Nine is about **communication** and ensures that life in the family and society is possible through the trust which comes from people speaking the truth and keeping their word. Economists agree that without trust and true communication, an economy cannot grow. Commandment Ten urges us to be thankful for what one has and to rejoice with what others have, avoiding unhealthy enmity which would again affect **family, economy, government** and **all other areas of life**.

We can see that the Law speaks into all areas of life. Thus in a godly nation, all gates of society are founded on the heart of God (the Law), building up on the family as the foundational unit of society (see more about family in chapter 5). All gates are connected to each other and reveal the character of God. Economy reveals God's provision, the church God's mercy, the media God's truth, education God's wisdom, government God's justice, science God's order and the arts God's order.

Here, we gave a summary of the Ten Commandments. We would like to encourage you to dig deeper! To do so, you can ask yourself the following four questions: (1) What did God command? (2) Why did God command this? (3) What are the good fruits of obedience (for me and the whole nation)? (4) What are the bad fruits of disobedience (for me and the whole nation)? In this way, you will get a deeper understanding of God's heart, the blessings we can have when we obey, and the problems and difficulties which come with disobedience towards God's law.

Jesus broke the Ten Commandments down into a simple summary: "You shall love the Lord your God with all your heart and with all your soul and with your entire mind. This is the great and first commandment. And a second is like it: You shall love your neighbor as yourself. On these two commandments depend all the Law and the Prophets"[22]. Paul

---

[22] Matt. 22:37-40

even reduced this further, saying: "For the whole law is fulfilled in one word: You shall love your neighbor as yourself."[23]. The entire law is about loving the people around us – the only way to restore our broken relationships as described in chapter 3. Giving the law was God's strategy to eliminate all causes of poverty among his chosen people!

Did God achieve His goal with Israel?

From the history of Israel, we have seen that God took many slaves out of Egypt, a poor people without any land. Then, he promised to make them a prosperous nation, a nation set high above all nations on earth, if they obeyed his commandments[24].

Did God fulfill this promise? Yes! Three hundred years after the Exodus, Israel was set above all nations. The peak of Israel was reached when Solomon was king. In 1 Kings 10 we read about the queen of Sheba's visit to Israel. She travelled from the far South[25] to see if what she heard about King Solomon's fame was true. After seeing and hearing with her own eyes, she testified the following: "The report was true that I heard in my own land of your words and of your wisdom, but I did not believe the reports until I came and my own eyes had seen it. And behold, the half was not told me. Your wisdom and prosperity surpass the report that I heard"[26]. And again 1 Kings 10:23 makes it clear: "Thus King Solomon excelled all the kings of the earth in riches and

---

[23] Gal. 5:14
[24] Deut. 28:1
[25] Mat. 12:42
[26] 1Kings10:6-7

in wisdom." Even Jesus referred to the glory of Solomon when he spoke about the most beautiful dressing in Matthews 6:29 – The promise of God had been fulfilled!

The Jews have been successful business people and scientists throughout their entire history. There are more Jewish noble prize winners than from any other nation[27]. Many of today's biggest companies were founded and are still led by Jews (as Google, Facebook and Starbucks, just to mention tree). In their entire history, people were always jealous of them and often tried to eliminate them. Their greatest persecution was during the time of Hitler, where about six million Jews were killed. But even when the Jews had to flee to other countries, they were established quickly and rose to influential positions, employing the people of their host country. Why? Their worldview had been shaped by the Law of God, which gave them a hope for this world and the understanding needed to be successful in every situation.

Nations today rise and fall depending on their worldview and the application of biblical truth. Before the reformation, in which the biblical principles were applied in society, Europe was poor. But from the time of the reformation, it mounted up and became prosperous. Today, however, many people in Europe despise the God of the bible and His word. This is why Europe is going down. The same happened with the United States. Its foundation was biblical, but now that people have taken the Bible from their courts, their businesses, their schools and all other areas of life, the United States is in big financial and social trouble. There are slums in the huge cities of America, in which people are experiencing greater poverty than the poor you find in Africa. For example, in Malawi, poor people still have their mud house

---

[27] http://www.ishitech.co.il/1204ar3.htm, 12.02.2013

and a piece of land to cultivate, while in the United States, they have neither land nor a mud house, but sleep in simple carton shelters. In conclusion, we can see that these biblical principles are really working. It does make a difference if you live them! The blessing, however, is not on the knowledge of the law, but on the application of it in everyday life.

The Individual

We learnt from God how he disciple Israel and trained them to be a great nation with strong economy. Since we are not God and cannot teach a whole nation at a time, the best place to start is to educate and individual in the laws of God. A single person's idea can transform a family, society and nation for good or for bad. To make a positive contribution to economy as an individual, firstly somebody needs to know who God is, as clearly seen in the commandments. It was to shape the worldview of the people towards reality. An individual has to know God's character, His nature and what He wants. Secondly an individual needs to know who man is, that man is fallen and sinful. This means that man is subject to failure and to making mistakes. Thus one needs direction and orientation in the world of business. This orientation we get from the bible. Thirdly an individual needs to know what truth is. This is the most important question, even in our generation today, because most people are confused about it. To build a stable economy, an individual needs to know what truth is. Economy cannot be built on falsehood. To take a biblical example, in John 18 Jesus was arrested and was brought before Pilate. There Jesus was asked by him: "Are you the king? Jesus answered, "You say rightly that I am a king. For this cause I was born and for this cause I have come into the world, that I should bear witness to the truth." Pilate then asked him: "What is truth?" Later Nietzsche, the German philosopher said that this question of Pilate is the most important point in the whole bible[28]. Before that time all philosophers had already given up the hope of knowing truth. So Pilate was shocked to hear that Jesus wants to testify about the truth. He was thinking: "how could this Galilean carpenter know the truth while all the philosophers say they don't know the truth? - Since truth cannot be discovered. Today we have exactly the same situation: truth is thought to be relative to one's own point of you. It cannot be imposed on others. Even Christians are affected by this view and choose what they like from the Bible and leave the verses they don't like. Thus the Bible has lost its power today. This understanding of truth causes problems to economy. Let's imagine somebody beliefs that stealing is wrong, but another thinks it's right because it is a good way for him to feed his family. How can economy work that way? The fourth point our responsibility towards the truth. If there is a truth which is absolute and true for everybody, then we all have the responsibility to live according to this truth. This way we will be able to build a strong economy.

In history we've got many examples how an individual can be a curse or a blessing to a nation or the whole world. A bad example is Adolf Hitler. He had a vision and a plan. He was inspired by Charles Darwin who came up with the theory of "the survival of the fittest". Being inspired by those writings, he got the inspiration that the Germans are a supreme race[29]. The end result of Hitler's ideology was chaos, hunger, and poverty. Thus it's our responsibility to train individuals to know who man is and the character of man and his inability to save

---

[28] Jan A. Aertsen, in: *Truth. Studies of a Robust Presence*, edited by Kurt Pritzl, p.130
[29] Weikart, 2004

himself. Sometimes we have bad ideas. That's why we always need to be under the moral authority of God. In the Bible we can read the story of a man who was very zealous to defend the truth as he believed it. Saul of Tarsus was a studied Pharisee and persecuted the early church – because he thought they were blaspheming God. But then he had an encounter with Jesus on the road to Damascus[30]. This changed his whole belief system and he became the most influential Apostle in history. In the same way individuals can still be transformed today through the revelation of Jesus Christ. Having this in mind, let us look at families and how a family can influence economy in the following.

---

[30] Acts 9

Chapter 5

Family – Cornerstone of Economy

A family is the smallest unit of society. The Greek word for family is 'oikos'. It is the same word from which the English word 'economy' comes from. Family and economy have much in common. Economy simply means the management or the stewardship of the household. The family produces or affects economy in one way or another. A household can contribute a lot to the well-being of the economy or can destroy it depending on its principles, values and choices. Economy also depends on the relationship between different families towards each other. Only through good interactions and honesty can the economy grow.

In the following, we look more closely at how the family can affect the economy and why the family is so important. We will be looking at the values of the family as a couple, the raising of children and how one household relates to others.

Values of a Couple

*I adjure you, O daughters of Jerusalem, by the gazelles
or the does of the field, that you not stir up or awaken
love until it pleases. (Songs 2:7)*

For couples to be strong, they have to follow the advice of
Solomon as quoted above: During their courtship, they need to
set clear boundaries that prevent them from having sex before
marriage. If the couple waits till they receive God's blessing in
the church, the marriage will be strong, because there will be
mutual trust between the two. Since they have shown that they
can control themselves before marriage, there will be trust
between the two, that each partner can control himself within
the marriage and stays faithful to the other, even if the two
have to separate for a time. If this advice is not followed,
economic problems will be created for the future. Your
partner will think: "what can keep my husband or wife from
having sex, while we are separated?" And in many families, it
has happened that one partner went away for business and
either or both were not faithful, because they could not
control their sex energy while separated. The consequence is
a broken family. This affects the economy, because separated
couples have more expenditure. Also, the children suffer and
might get on the wrong track, which would lead them into
poverty.

Another important value is the view of the roles of husband
and wife. In our world today, we can observe two opposing
extremes in view of this topic that are both not biblical and
consequently, lead to poverty. There is one culture that takes
the scripture from Genesis 3:16 where God says to the
woman, "Your desire shall be for your husband, and he shall
rule over you." They emphasize that the husband has to rule

over their wife, and are convinced that this is the will of God. Thus, they chain their wife at home and don't allow her to have even a small business. The potential of the woman is suppressed and her ability to create wealth dies.

The other extreme is the culture that emphasizes the equality of man and woman, since they are both equally created in the image of God[31]. They interpret this scripture in a way that man and woman are so equal that they have the same responsibilities. In this case, the woman is expected to work full time like the husband. The problem in this case is that the children are given to a day care center and are not receiving character training from their parents. If they develop a bad character due to the absence of their parents, they will mismanage their resources and end up in poverty. What then is the biblical interpretation of the role of man and woman? As so often in other cases, it is the balance between the two extremes. The abusive hierarchical structure which we see today and was part of the curse in Gen. 3 came as a result of man's rebellion against God. The most fundamental principle for the biblical family is love. The husband has to love his wife and the wife has to submit to her husband in love[32]. Nobody can say that he loves the invisible God but fails to live in peace with his wife. Many families fail because they say: "God first, then family, then ministry". But in practice this cannot work. If one says God first, but ministry third, who's ministry is it? God's or man's? These three things are going together, they are not hierarchical. The way you love God reflects how you love

---

[31] Gen. 1:27
[32] Eph. 4

your wife or husband and the way you love your spouse reflects the way you love God. This is a critical point, because we even saw pastors divorced, because they said the wife was a hindrance to their ministry. So they decided to divorce their wife so that they can serve God better. Then their children get bitter, because their parents divorced because of God. Later it will negatively affect economy, because they don't believe in marriage anymore.

Since man and woman were created differently (man outside the garden, woman inside), they have different responsibilities in the family; however, this does not affect their equality. Since Jesus has come and redeemed us from the power of the curse, we cannot take the curse and keep imposing it as the standard of how to run a family. This means the woman does not have to stay at home the whole time or be a slave of the man, but that she can use her creativity to create wealth. On the other hand, she is still responsible for her home and has to be there for her children. She cannot work full time, if the husband is working as well. There has to be an agreement between the couple that decides who will be at home to take care of the children and who is going to work. If both are working, they shouldn't do so at the same time. While one is working, the other has to be with the children and vice versa. It this way, the children will not miss anything and can develop a godly character that will help them manage their resources. In doing so, their business will prosper and they can become all God wanted them to be. The goal is that everyone will be empowered. Strong women who are empowered by the freedom of the law of God are able to bring up strong children. Strong children then grow up into strong women and men again.

Bad versus good environment for children

The foundation of a strong family is a strong marriage. If the parents love each other and are faithful to each other, they produce a good environment for their children. The most important way the children can learn to be faithful and trust others, is by seeing it from their parents. It is best for them to experience honesty from their parents and learn that their parents keep their word. But some parents can even train their children to lie! The following example illustrates this:

There was a family which had some credits to pay. Because they failed to keep their word the creditors came to their house to get the money. But the parents hid themselves in their room and told the children to tell the creditors that they are not at home.

Actions are more powerful than words! If the children learn to lie in their family they might very well do the same in their future and destroy the economy!

Also, a family in constant conflict produces a bad environment for children. Conflicts come for different reasons. Something that significantly affects the family is unfaithfulness between the couple in the area of sexual purity. When the man or the woman has other sexual partners, the end result is divorce in most cases. This is why God forbids adultery and divorce. If the parents' divorce, the children grow up with a single parent. Statistics show that children from single parents have more problems in school and are more violent[33]. Divorce weakens the next generations. It can even affect the family of the child in the future. What the child learned from the parents

---

[33] American Academy of Children and Adolescent Psychiatry, http://www.aacap.org/cs/root/facts_for_families/understanding_violent_beh avior_in_children_and_adolescents 12.02.2013

is that the solution to disagreements is to run away. They are lacking in conflict management. This is probably the reason for higher violence rates, even in youths.

There are Christian parents who go to church every Sunday and send their children to Sunday school. At home, they even pray with the children and read to them from the bible. Yet, their lifestyle is not consistent with what they teach their children. Maybe the parents fight often in the presence of their children, or maybe they are abusive, or have addictions that affect the family life. Later, they may wonder why the children are not continuing in the way of the Lord or are not successful in their business. What the parents missed is that actions are more powerful than words. Children learn more from what they experience than from what is taught. If they grow up in an insecure environment, they will be insecure in their business and cannot invest well because of fear.

Raising children for a successful life

How can parents produce a good environment for their children to be successful in the world of economy? The most important way parents can teach their children is by showing, through example, a loving attitude and how to walk in obedience to God. The children first have to know that they are loved. Then, they will understand that God loves them. They also have to learn to obey, so they can submit to authorities and, more importantly, to God. These are the two fundamental principles through which the parents can reflect the character of God to their children.

In order for children to learn these two lessons, they need the presence of both parents. Your presence is more profitable than money! If one is absent from the home, how can children know that both parents love them? And how can they learn to be obedient? Many fathers today are absent because they go far away for better work. The children do not need money from South Africa, but the presence of the father. If someone wants to go to South Africa or the UK, he or she has to go with the whole family. In this way, neither the marriage nor the children will suffer. But many destroy both – marriage and children – in order to have more money. Most of the time, however, they are not better off working abroad. We know people personally who went abroad and left their family behind. First, they sent some money home, but then they stopped because they found another partner. The problem was that through the distant relationship, their love to their marriage partner diminished, and they looked for love from another source. In the attempt to become prosperous, their family ended up in greater poverty. A friend of ours used to say "building relationships is more important than making lots of money".

The goal parents need to keep in mind, is to raise the children in a loving and secure environment where they get trained practically to know good and evil and to make good choices. This is the foundation that they need in order to face the world with confidence and to be successful in economy once they are grown. As Proverbs 22:6 puts it: "Train up a child in the way he should go; even when he is old he will not depart from it". If the parents draw clear boundaries for the children and discipline them, they will learn that their behavior can have good or bad consequences. In this way, they are trained to become self-responsible. This will help the children to also be responsible in their business by making the right choices. If they know how to build and maintain good relationships and have a good character are on the best way to create wealth!

Relations between Households

You shall not covet your neighbour's house; you shall not covet your neighbour's wife, or his male servant, or his female servant, or his ox, or his donkey, or anything that is your neighbour's.
(Ex.20:17)

How does one household affect others in terms of economy? Anyone would agree that he doesn't want to start a business next to the house of a thief. Likewise, no one wants to have a business partner that wants to win his partner's wife or husband. This is why God proclaimed in the Ten Commandments that we should not covet anything that belongs to our neighbor. We do not want to be close to such a family who is known for coveting everything someone else has. We will feel insecure next to them and always be suspicious of them. We will ask, what will be the end result of their covetousness? Will they act upon their desires and destroy my business or take my wife? Or do I even have to fear for my life, since they are so jealous of me?

From this example of a covetous family, we can understand the tremendous effect values and principles of one family have on other families. To take this thought a bit further, let's imagine a country where covetousness is common. It will be very difficult to prosper in this environment. Every step one takes to advance, to improve his or her business, will be attacked by people who cannot stand seeing their neighbors growing bigger than themselves. The productivity of such a country would be very limited, since no one could reach his or her potential, while always being stopped by those around them.

Let's turn this example around and ask the question, what would a country look like where most households valued private property and were determined to respect what belonged to others? If no one even thought of taking what was not his, but wanted to help others grow as well? In such an environment, personal efforts in businesses would be encouraged and economy would prosper.

Chapter 6

The 5 Gates that influence Economy

In the previous chapter we have been looking at the family as the cornerstone of economy. Now we are looking at five gates that influence economy. In the Bible we have verses which give us an idea of what a gate is: it was the place where all business was transacted[34]. It was also the place where every public communication was made[35] and causes were decided. The gates were the most important place in the ancient cities. Jesus picked up the teaching of the gates in the New Testament in Mat. 16: 18: "On this rock, I will build my church and the *gates* of hell shall not prevail against it." In our study about Poverty and Alternative Economy, we cannot ignore the important gates which can influence the development of economy in one way or another. In the following we are going to look at the church gate, the education gate, the government gate, the science gate and finally the media, arts and entertainment gate.

---

[34] Gen. 23:10
[35] Gen. 34:20

Church – The Agent of Change

The church is the agent of mercy and love and it is the window through which the world should see God's intentions now. If you have never experienced love and you don't know what love is, you need to know it in the community first. So if the church does not demonstrate love honesty and mercy, people cannot learn these things on their own. Through the church people should see love, honesty and mercy manifested.

John Wesley taught ten thousand small-group leaders in honest and godly living to train new converts[36]. Before Wesley the state of England was terrible. There was prostitution and stealing. The girls were getting married by the time they were 13 years old. Our duty is that the church needs to be reformed. If somebody is reformed, the heart is reformed. Honesty and godly living as John Wesley taught. The same happened in Geneva. It was the smelliest city of Switzerland, but John Calvin started to train the people to be honest, to work hard and do something profitable instead of drinking. He taught the husbands to be faithful to their wives. And now Geneva is an important diplomatic city. There are the UN and the Red Cross. But it all started with the people of the church to bring a positive influence to society and the nation at large. The church is the place where politicians, bankers, lawyers and many more people from different walks of life meet. This is the opportunity of the leaders of the church to train the people in honesty in businesses and at their workplace in general. Most of the time we see that churches are not reformed and what we see is competition: which church is bigger? If we can analyze the message which is being taught in the church it is the whole year about faith and love from different angels. But people are not

---

[36] Cunningham, 2007

trained on how to live daily. This creates problems in the world of economy, because the people are not equipped to live honest. If the church can start preparing its' members for the challenges in the world, and how to be Christians at their workplace, in their business, in politics, we can build strong economy and then great nations. If the churches still continue to be weak without having any focus, it will be difficult or impossible to develop sustainable or strong economy. It is our sincere desire in this book to challenge the body of Christ to wake up and take our responsibility which has been given to us by good: to be the window and the lampstand in the world through which people can see God's intentions in our daily living as Paul put it in Ephesians 3:10: "so that through the church the manifold wisdom of God might now be made known to the rulers and authorities in the heavenly places." The church is the agent of order in the society. And it's the only institution chosen by God which can bring real transformation.

Education

"In any society, education should be for the enhancement of the people, for the development of the individual until they become a source of help and blessing to humanity. Education should prepare a man to be able to serve his community and humanity, bringing to the table his own quota in meeting the economic, social, intellectual, and spiritual needs of his nation and of the world."
(Ashimolowo, 2007, p.289)

As much as the world has vast and diverse resources, nothing can be compared with the human mind and creativity. This potential can be unlocked through education. Thus a nation and economics can only develop if people value education and if it is made available to commoners. A recent example where this happened is South Korea[37]. But what do you teach? Firstly one needs to learn the skills to read and write. From there one can learn knowledge and form his character. Once somebody is able to read, he or she can read the word of God which transforms lives and economy. It was through the availability of the Bible in the language of the people and the biblical teachings of the reformers which resulted in a flourishing economy in Switzerland and Germany in the 16th century. Unfortunately, today the character is often neglected in education. This brings up a destructive danger, which reminds us of Roosevelt's famous statement: "A man who has never gone to school may steal from a freight car; but if he has a university education, he may steal the whole railroad."

This destructiveness of knowledge without character can also be seen in the more recent film "Social Network" which shows how Mark Zuckerberg became a 23 old Billionaire by cheating everybody, including his best friends. The Harvard University had given him knowledge and skills, but no character.

Coming back to the entry quote to this topic, a pupil going to school should learn relevant things which help him or her to live a balanced life: to have the wisdom to make good decisions, to know how to relate to other people, to God and how to contribute to economy. In the Bible we can learn how people can become great and a blessing to others. God chose Abraham so that he should teach his children to walk in the way of God by doing righteousness and justice[38]. For the economy to work today it needs people who are committed to righteousness and justice. Pupils also need to learn to have vision and purpose for their nation. Further it's very important

---

[37] Cunningham, 2007
[38] Gen. 18:19

that pupils learn to be honest. Without integrity a nation and its economy cannot stand. All these principles need to be installed in the curriculums of schools. If this is not the case in our country, we need to adapt the curriculum, so that the pupils learn to serve their society in all areas. Wisdom is needed so that high officials in politics cannot take advantage of ignorant people. In Malawi, for example, politicians take advantage of the people in the villages that are not educated. They propagate something which the uneducated don't know about and use deceiving propaganda to get people behind them. To achieve the development of a person as a whole people who know the Triune God of the Bible need to involved in curriculum formulation in our nations. This is also a key of the Muslims. They influence and change the curriculum of a nation and change its history to achieve their purposes. Even if we Christians are confused about how we can take influence in education, Muslims are not.

Government

"Good governance includes the creation, protection, and enforcement of property rights, without which the scope for market transactions is limited. It includes the provision of a regulatory regime that works with the market to promote competition. And it includes the provision of sound macroeconomic policies that create a stable environment for the market activity. Good governance also means the absence of corruption, which can subvert the goals of politics and undermine the legitimacy of public institutions that support the market"
(The World Bank, in: Mutharika, p. 184))

As much as the family is the cornerstone of economy, governance is the hub which holds all things together. The goal of any government should be to create the environment in which sustainable economic growth can take place. It should also aim on controlling the inflation of the country's currency and support the creating of job opportunities for its citizens so that the unemployment rate is at a low level. Furthermore, the government is responsible for creating a healthy balanced payment system and should be able to control its spending and borrowing from other nations. In our travels and studies from books and world news, it's evident that without good governance, the goals above cannot be reached. Political instability brings chronicle poverty among the nation.

Alternative Economy as described in this book is founded on God's word which reveals that people are fallen and power has to be limited. Thus a country can develop better, if it has the concept of power division in judicative, executive and legislative[39].

In the Indiana Jones film Raiders of the Lost Ark (1981) the American and the Nazi armies are trying to find the Ark of the Covenant. The American agents were worried, because they thought that the ones who find the ark first will have power. They thought it was the ark which made the armies of Israel invincible. But the question is: what was in the ark? In the ark were the two tablets of stone which contain the ten commandments of God. In the film, the Americans got the Ark before the Germans, but in actual sense the German speakers found the ark first. Through the translation and teachings of Luther they got the commandments of God in their own language and it helped them to become the greatest nations on

---

[39] Cunningham, 2007

earth. . Later also the British had a reformation because the bible was translated into the language of the people. Through the word of God people learnt to be honest and to keep their word. In the history of Israel, Moses, David and Solomon put the Ark of the Covenant into the heart of the nation. These stories show that a nation can develop if they have the understanding that they need something which transcends human knowledge. This understanding that we have a God which has spoken and that he gave rules which are above human beings was for masters and slaves alike: "You shall not kill, you shall not covet." That's why the prophets could go to Ahab and aks him: Why did you kill Nabot?[40] - Because there is a law which says one should not kill and covet. But if there is no law above the kings, they kill whom they want to kill and spared whom they wanted to spare. That's how it was with the pharaohs in Egypt. – And still today in Africa, leaders are often above the law. Through that nations get destroyed, because man is fallen and gets corrupted by power. The result is bad laws which hinder economic development and trap many people in poverty. Because man is fallen, checks and balances need to be woven into the political system. In Switzerland the national government is in Bern, but the High Court is in Lausanne. Switzerland made this division in the time of Reformation when they put the Bible at the foundation of their government.

Or how did America become great? The Puritans, the founding fathers of America saw themselves as building the New Jerusalem. They committed themselves to keeping God's laws; America then grew and became the greatest nation on earth. But now it is going away from the biblical foundation and therefore resembles a sinking ship. The laws of God are the important function in building great nations. But today even

---

[40] 1 Kings 21

Christians have a misunderstanding of God's law. Some say, we don't live in the time of the law, but in the time of grace alone. The question is then: How do you build a nation on grace? We celebrate amazing grace, but nobody celebrates amazing truth. In John 1:17 it's written that: "The law was given through Moses, but grace and truth came through Jesus Christ." How do you come to truth? By knowing what is right and wrong. And this you know through the law. Today, Evangelicals often are confused about this. That's one of the problems of America today and some other nations. The dispensationalists say we are in the time of grace and the time of law is passed. Because of this belief they left the law faculty to the secular institutions. There were no more Christian law faculties and institutes. Now the majorities of layers and judges think and judge from a secular and humanistic point of view.

To build great nations with economic prosperity, it's important that the government passes good legislations which give every citizen an equal share in the development of the nation. For the poor and the rich alike, the starting of a new business has to be made possible. Further government offices should be evenly distributed across the country so that every area has got access to important offices with services in the area of immigration issues, business registrations etc.

Every citizen needs to know the laws of the nation and to have a fair hearing and defense in the courts and the chance to appeal. As Deut. 1:9-17 puts it when Moses instructed the judges that they need to hear everybody alike and the difficult causes should go to the high court (Moses). Moses is also showing the important point that people should be involved in choosing their leaders who can represent them. Their qualities should be wise, understanding and experienced men.

Democracy

"The truths of the Judeo-Christian tradition are infinitely precious, not only, as I believe, because they are true, but also because they provide the moral impulse which alone can lead to that peace, in the true meaning of the word, for which we all long...there is little hope for democracy if the hearts of men and women in democratic societies cannot be touched by a call to something greater than themselves. Political structures, state institutions, collective ideals are not enough...[Democracy requires] the life of faith...as much to the temporal as to the spiritual welfare of the nation."
(British Prime Minister Margarat Thatcher)

In our world today and in most African countries, we can observe that democracy is used as a vehicle for the majority to manipulate the rights of the minority. This can be clearly observed in Muslim societies where the Muslim Brotherhood come to power through democracy and then force the Sharia law on everybody. As a result there is political instability and poverty.

What is democracy? Abraham Lincoln, the 16th US President said in 1863: "Democracy is the government of the people, by the people, for the people." Based on this quote, for a democracy to work, the people should participate in important decisions of the nation. But if people don't have one common reference point and belief system, it is difficult to build a just and stable society. Everybody will just have his or her own view which brings instability whereby investors will be scared away. This can be clearly observed in the nations in which there is political instability now, as in Egypt, Syria and Mali, just to mention a few. People are in poverty and depend on humanitarian aid. In any democracies, the understanding of the

Judeo-Christian worldview is critical for peace, stability and rule of law in the nation. Without this it will not be possible to have a functioning democracy in our world. Today we experience that once a party has won the elections, the opposition parties start to do everything to bring that party in a bad light so that they can win the next elections. They can even refuse good laws and vote for bad laws just to frustrate the efforts of the ruling government. This behavior is a result of greed and pride and shows how far we have moved away from our Judeo-Christian roots.

In the light of all this, we can clearly observe that good governance is indeed the hub which holds the society together in providing peace and stability and creating a stable environment for businesses to thrive. And this can only happen on basis of the biblical understanding of reality.

Science

The earth is an open system. Development is about discovering and exploring God's world. It's not just about helping people to survive. It's about creating new resources, not just about redistributing scarce ones. Thus the world is only limited by our own creativity and stewardship (Miller). We can make research and create things. Through our creativity – because we are made in the image of God – we will be able to build great nations, to develop. Because man started in the garden, but revelation shows us the end as a city. In between we need human creativity. Discovering things and making things. And because the Jews had hope for this world they discovered a lot. It was Jews who invented the telephone, polio vaccine and are now working on an HIV vaccine. We have been given the mind to do research. But because of wrong understandings in the church Christians were afraid to engage more in science. The church surrendered its dominance and said, we are just a faith community. Whenever something could not be discovered, they said it's a mystery of God. But the first scientists were Christians and the studied the world based on the conviction that they live in a logical universe, because God has made it. In the beginning there was the word (logos) and there is order and patterns in the universe. Through that science is being used to bless people and to liberate them from the curse of toil. There are some works which are to be done by animals or machines, but still people are doing them. Through science people get liberated and receive their humanness[41]. We need people who are Christians and involve in Science to discover vaccines and improve crop varieties for agriculture and to find good ways of overcoming hunger and poverty. These people should have the fear of God and thus don't just discover things for their own profit, but as a blessing for the nations. Unfortunately drugs and new innovations are so expensive today, that the poor cannot access them – which makes the gap between the rich and the poor even bigger. Through the proper use of science and technology we will be able to build a strong and stable economy. We will find better ways of growing crops, better ways of crafting fruit trees and better ways of fighting diseases in humans and animals. The nations should aim on training their own scientists. Any nation who depends on scientists from other nations to develop cures, finds it hard to afford to pay for their discoveries. And instead of creating work opportunities and wealth in the nation, the money flows to another and the local people don't profit. Then the nation becomes dependent on others and is not self-sustaining and self-supporting.

---

[41] Mangalwadi, 2011

Arts, Media and Entertainment

Most of the people have little understanding how arts, media and entertainment can influence peoples thinking and the choices they will make in the near future. Others might be aware of it, but don't give it much attention. If you want to know how the next generation is going to live and behave, just listen to the new music, watch the advertisements on TV and on the internet. These musicians, artist and advertisers somehow act like prophets of our time

This is the most influential gate which can build or destroy economy in our nations. TV, radio, internet and films are so powerful, because discipleship takes place unnoticed. Every film producer and advertiser has got a message which he wants people to belief. The sad thing is that this gate is often controlled by secular people and as a result of that we get indoctrinated with biased information and distorted worldviews which are not in line with the truth. If we would have Christians in influential places in the media who are committed to tell true stories with the right worldview, how would our programs and films look today? What would be presented? We would have more films that honor God and encourage people to live righteous. In America, for example, there is a church that is producing films with powerful messages. Their second film is called "Courageous" and is not just thrilling to watch, but changes the lives of many people toward loving God and their families. But if we leave the whole media to the secular, they will disciple our children. Madonna, when she gives a concert somewhere and dances in front of many youth what is she doing? She is discipling them. Jesus told us to go out and make disciples[42], but if we don't do that, then the world will disciple

---

[42] Mat. 28

us with its message and agendas. If you see pornographic pictures and people having sex or walking half naked on the street. What does it teach you? That this is normal and part of our culture today? But what was God's response to Adam when he was naked and hiding? God killed an animal and covered their nakedness[43]. This can give you an idea of what God thinks about sinful people being naked. As a result of the nakedness today we also see much rape, fornication and adultery. It is different with the time in Gen. 2:24 when Adam and Eve were both naked and not ashamed. That was before the fall – there was no sin and because of that it was not dangerous to be naked. Even king David in the Bible was tempted to sin not only committed adultery, but even murder, just because of seeing a naked woman.

But what is the connection with economy? This destructive behavior with fornication and rape is very expensive. There are unwanted pregnancies which call for abortion and children growing up in broken families which weaken economy.

What if we could use media, entertainment and advertisement to promote the beauty and the abundant resources of our nation which God has given us? It will attract investors to start businesses.

When we went to Malawi with a British architect, he didn't have many days in Malawi, but we showed him Lake Malawi which is the third largest lake of Africa. He was thrilled and surprised to see the beauty and he asked me: Why can we not hear about Malawi in the international News and get advertisements for holidays at the beautiful Lake of Malawi? But what they show on the news is only the Nyawu dancers (traditional: Big Dance, which in my interpretation is connected to witchcraft) and poverty. That one time visit to Malawi by

---

[43] Gen. 3

this British architect has created a longing desire in him to return.

What if we use media in the right way and advertise that 70 to 80 % of all aquarium fish in Europe come from Lake Malawi? - Instead of allowing bad pictures to dominate in order for organizations to raise more funds. What if we communicated the truth and said that many natural resources which are processed and sold in Europe come from Africa? We would create more jobs and attract investors and boost economy.

Chapter 7

Principles of Alternative Economy

We mentioned already that family and economy have much in common, as they both come from the same Greek word 'oikos'. In this chapter, we will focus on economy. Economy, however, is a wide field. There are two branches: microeconomics and macroeconomics. Microeconomics is "the study of how households and firms make decisions and how they interact in markets."[44] Macroeconomics is "the study of economy-wide phenomena, including inflation, unemployment and economic growth." In this study, we focus on microeconomics, as it is the part of economy which we can directly apply in our lives, while macroeconomics deals more with national and world economy as a whole. A university economics text book starts with the following definition: "Economics is the study of how society manages its scarce resources."[45] Where does this scarcity of resources

---

[44] Mankiw & Taylor, 2006
[45] Mankiw & Taylor, 2006

come from? It is from a worldview that is not biblical. We are made in the image of God, who is a creator, and we have the ability to create. We have the capacity to multiply things. We are not in a closed system. There is no limit to increase! That's why the Jews are successful, they have understood this truth.

When we read the first book of the bible, Genesis, we read that God commanded Adam: "Be fruitful and multiply and fill the earth and subdue it and have dominion over the fish of the sea and over the birds of the heavens and over every living thing that moves on the earth"[46]. God wanted Adam to multiply and to increase. And in Deut. 8:18 it is written that it is "the LORD your God...who gives you power (capacity, ability, strength, substance) to get (do, make) wealth". To be part of an economy, you have to produce goods and services. How can we do that successfully? We have to start thinking like economists. How do they think? There are five principles which we will discuss in detail:

- Vision
- Observation & Strategizing
- Knowledge
- Commitment
- Investment

---

[46] Gen. 1:28

Vision

> *Where there is no vision (mental sight; dream,*
> *revelation), the people perish; but*
> *he who keeps the law, he is blessed.*
> *(Prov. 29:18)*

What is the definition of a vision? The Cambridge Dictionary, 2007 defines 'vision' as follows:

Having a vision is the ability to imagine how a country, society, industry, etc. could develop in the future and to plan in a suitable way.

Having a vision for the economy is very important. It gives you the foundation for what you want to do and achieve in the area of economics. In science, this is called a theory. It is the basis on which a scientist conducts experiments. In the same way, we need to have a vision to be successful economically. Even the bible tells us that without vision, people perish. What do you think about the future? Where do you see yourself in five or ten years? Do you see yourself in the same situation you are in today? Every successful company starts with a vision. Based on this vision, investment plans can be made. Let's look at a biblical example: The story of Joshua and the city of Jericho. Because they feared the Israelites, the inhabitants of Jericho closed all their gates. When the children of Israel arrived at Jericho, the first thing God told Joshua was: "See, I have given Jericho into your hand, with its king and mighty men of valour"[47]. Here, we learn something about the power of imagination. Joshua had to imagine (see!) and know that it was theirs, so that they could get it later. If Joshua did not see that God gave them Jericho, they could not have possessed it!

---

[47] Jos. 6:2

Vision determines how far you can go in life and how much you can accomplish. If you imagine only small things you cannot reach bigger ones. If you want to make a difference in your situation now, you better start dreaming big! This is why God told Abraham: "The LORD said to Abram, after Lot had separated from him, 'Lift up your eyes and look from the place where you are, northward and southward and eastward and westward, for all the land that you see I will give to you and to your offspring forever'"[48]. Abraham had to imagine what he was going to posses from where he was. How far you go in life is determined by how far you see! This leads us to the next point, which is observation and strategizing.

Observation & Strategizing

Economists think like scientists. While other people simply accept things as they are, economists try to find solutions. They make observations in their community to find out which goods or services are lacking, in order to discover new business opportunities. Then, they come up with strategies and ideas on how to start new businesses. To illustrate this principle we have a short illustration below:

Two shoe makers went into a village to observe whether there was a need for shoes, so that they could take advantage of the market. While they both made the same observation that these villagers all walked barefoot, they came up with two different conclusions. The one said to himself that he cannot sell any shoes, because no one is used to wearing shoes here. The other one saw that if he could prove to the people the importance and practical need of shoes in daily life, there would be a huge opportunity to market his produce.

---

[48] Gen 13:14-15

We see that the latter had the mentality of a true economist, while the first one didn't.

As we mentioned before, we have the ability from God to be creative. We need to use this creativity when we want to be successful economically. To apply our creativity, however, we have to observe what is already there, and see what future possibilities can be created by opening up new markets.

Acquiring Knowledge

Blessed is the one who finds wisdom, and the one who gets understanding, for the gain from her is better than gain from silver and her profit better than gold. (Prov. 3:13-14)

In every field we want to engage, we need knowledge. If you have interest in economics, you have to educate yourself. Choose the area in which you want to become active and start making a survey: ask people with experience in this field, try to find common strengths and weaknesses and find ways to improve. The goal is to come up with something unique which has not yet been there and also solve a present problem of people.

Many times, people want to start the same business they see their neighbors have. But this doesn't work. If everyone has the same, there are only sellers and no more customers. The best way is for people in the same community to have different businesses, so that they can all exchange their goods and services to the profit of everyone.

It is dangerous to start a business without having enough knowledge in that area. For example, if you want to sell computers without knowing how they work, what they can do, what processer they have, how strong the battery is, or what kind of programs are on them, people will cheat you. The solution is to educate yourself well, find a mentor who can help you and maybe even attend a seminar!

The stronghold in the minds of some people is that they think they know everything already. They block their way to success. Wise people are always open to new ideas and counsel. They make new friendships with people who can help them grow in a certain area and are good listeners.

If you have a business that involves paying taxes, you have to know exactly how much to pay for what. As Jesus asked: "For which of you, desiring to build a tower, does not first sit down and count the cost, whether he has enough to complete it?"[49]. When you calculate all the costs well, you won't be cheated by officers, and won't make a loss. Some people are abused due to lack of knowledge. Do not just run to import something from Tanzania or South Africa without knowing the regulations. Educate yourself: how does it work? What are the things to consider? Inquire from faithful sources. Read the regulations and laws of your country by yourself and do not depend on the words of other business people who want to discourage you and make you depend on them.

Commitment

> *Do you not know that in a race all the runners run,*
> *but only one receives the prize? So run that you*
> *may obtain it. (1Cor. 9:24)*

A new business venture needs commitment. You have to be ready to sacrifice in the beginning. The start is always hard and slow. You can't start with much profit. Sometimes, you will not even gain anything at the beginning. First, you have to inform yourself and learn everything needed. During this

---

[49] Luk. 14:28

time you are not paid! But the Bible assures us: "It is the hard-working farmer who ought to have the first share of the crops"[50]
.

You have to make a commitment in order to be successful and not be discouraged. People often get discouraged in the beginning and change the business before they have really started. In this way, they can never increase. The customers will be confused because they will find you selling groundnuts on one day and fish on the other. When they will come to you again on the third day to buy fish, you want to sell clothes. When they finally come for clothes, you sell eggs. You need to have a clear vision and walk in it! Make a decision and let it be final. Be like a scientist; when they work on a project, they won't stop until they succeed, even if it takes time and brings no profit until it is finished. Thomas Edison, who made two thousand new inventions, of which the most famous was the light bulb, failed many times. Every time he failed, he was encouraged. He thought of each failure as one more way the light bulb doesn't work. Other people take failure personally and think they are not good enough for anything. But you are not a failure; it is only the method you used which failed! Be your best motivator. If you wait for people to encourage you, it will not work, because no one thinks like you and no one shares the same interest.

Investment
Economy is always connected to investment. Think like an economist who continually makes plans on how and where he can invest best. If you don't have a vision already and you have some money, you will just eat it. The first thing economists think when they get money into their hands, is

---

[50] 2 Tim. 2:6

how they can invest and multiply it. While somebody without an economist's mind just thinks of how to spend it.

Investment is important because it gives you the opportunity to multiply and increase your influence over time. Whenever you make a profit, you invest it until your money works for you while you are asleep. Successful people work smart, while others just work hard without getting enough. What we mean by working smart is to know how and when to invest in what. We want to encourage you to always think of how to reinvest your profit. If you just think of how to spend your profit and buy a satellite TV that comes with monthly bills or a car or mortgage you cannot increase. These things will start eating your capital instead.

As we live in the world of consumerism, we have to be careful not to catch the spirit of always wanting the newest products. The advertisements make needs out of wants by suggesting to us that we really need the advertised product. Before we saw that advertisement, however, we didn't have the idea that we would ever need such a product. This is how people get into debt. Our piece of advice is: if there is something that you won't need for the whole year, it is not worth buying. Some people want to buy new clothes or suits while they have a wardrobe full of clothes at home that they haven't used the whole year. Think of investment first! We will come back to this principle when we discuss how to start a business.

Chapter 8

Principles of Finance

When we talk about finance, it's about money management. In this chapter, we are going to discuss what money is, look at the universal principle of capital and profit, taken from the bible, and address the topic of credits and debt management on the basis of biblical principles.

Money

What is money? Money is a medium of exchange. What is a banknote? What distinguishes a banknote from another piece of paper? A banknote represents value. It does not have value in itself. The value comes from the agreement within a nation to use these kinds of banknotes to exchange goods. If I come from another nation, I first have to exchange my currency with the one used in my host country. It is not possible to use Malawian money in Switzerland. There, it is without value – just a piece of paper. Only the bank can exchange it and send it back to the original nation. But a bank can also refuse and say they don't exchange this kind of currency.

Banknotes are valuable because of convention and the signature on them that shows their acceptance. They cannot be produced by any unauthorized party, which is why they have a special seal. Even the government cannot produce money whenever they feel like it. When they produce too much, it causes inflation which means that the currency loses value. Why is that? Money is simply a representation of work and resources. If you work for a company, you get your salary as a representation of the work you did. Or when you sell your cotton, you receive money as a representation of your work you did to cultivate and harvest it.

If this were not so, the government could just print money and distribute it to the needy to solve the problem of poverty. But by doing so, they would destroy the whole economy because all the money in the country would lose its value. That's what happened in Zimbabwe in past years. Because the government was in debt, they produced more money, which resulted in poverty among the people, because the money halved its value almost every hour and food prices doubled again and again.

Today, paper money is replaced more and more by digital figures. People's salaries are going straight to their bank account, and they receive a printed receipt which shows them the amount of money they have. Instead of paying in the shops with paper money or coins, people pay with debit or credit cards. And when they pay bills, they use e-banking, where they type the figure they have to send, and it is removed from their bank account.

This change from money as paper and coins to digital figures allows us to better understand that banknotes and coins have no value in themselves, but are a representation of the work one does. The solution is then: if you want more money, you have to work more or be smarter or produce products of higher quality!

Capital & Profit

Every business works with capital and profit. But what is capital and what are the biblical principles about capital and profit? Let's look at a scripture from Deuteronomy:

> If you come across a bird's nest in any tree or on the ground, with young ones or eggs and the mother sitting on the young or on the eggs, you shall not take the mother with the young. You shall let the mother go, but the young you may take for yourself that it may go well with you and that you may live long. (Deut. 22:6-7)

From this scripture, we see the heart of God is interested in continuity. He doesn't want us to destroy the variety of animals he created by our mismanagement.

At the same time, we can learn several principles for business management. The mother bird is like the production capacity or the capital, while the eggs are the increase or the profit. So what is the definition of capital? Capital is something which has the capacity to produce a profit. Is money capital? Not necessarily! First, it is a profit. Money does not have the capacity to produce something. Real capitals are rather the following:

Tab. 1: Different Kinds of Capital

Examples of capital	Way of increase
Land	Something can be cultivated (profit: agricultural product), A house can be built (profit: rent)
Physical strength	Labor (profit: wages, salary)
Know-how/skills	Making new products out of raw material (= adding value). Example: making a table out of wood, bricks out of mud, and threads out of cotton. Selling a service: teaching computer skills
Animal	Goats, sheep, chicken: reproduce

We will look closer at the use of capital and profit when we discuss the topic of starting a business later on.

Credits & debt management

Under this topic, we are going to discuss what the Bible says about lending and borrowing of money. There are several scriptures in Deuteronomy about this subject. Let's look at some of them:

> If among you, one of your brothers should become poor, in any of your towns within your land that the LORD your God is giving you, you shall not harden your heart or shut your hand against your poor brother, but you shall open your hand to him and lend him sufficient for his need, whatever it may be.
> (Deut.
> 15:7-8)

Do lend if need be! Debt is not in principle evil or prohibited. But in what occasions should we lend or ask someone if we can borrow from him or her? This scripture clearly shows to whom you should lend: to a brother who has fallen into a situation from which he cannot stand up again. This can be through a catastrophe in his family or a sickness. It is somebody who is really in need and not just wanting a new car. It has to be someone you know (brother) and who lives in your country. Therefore, it is someone you know very well. It is within a community which grants the lender accountability. If the borrower does not pay back the money, other people of the same community are witnesses that he owes you. To this category of people the bible commands us to open our hearts.

Because the Bible says lending, it means lending and not giving! This means that the person who borrowed the money must have a plan to pay the money back.

What should be the purpose of the lent money? It is to cover essentials needs. It also creates the ability to generate more money, including the pay back. You cannot just go and borrow money to buy maize to eat without increasing it and thus having a plan to pay it back. That's stealing and not borrowing! You will have to start lying and finding excuses about when you are giving the money back. While the lender has to be generous, the borrower has to be faithful. God is concerned with both – the rights of the lender and the borrower!

Credits and financial crisis

From the scripture above, we learned lending is only for people in need. It is their way of standing up and supporting themselves again. Today, however, many people get credits to fulfill their wants and dreams, devastating the economy. The recent financial crisis, for example, happened because people in the United States were so deeply in debt due to abuse of credit cards. By fulfilling their wants, the whole bank system broke down. Because of globalization, this crisis extended into the whole world. The rich lost huge sums of money they had invested, and the commoners lost their jobs. The only solution for recovery from this financial crisis is the change of our attitude and behavior with money. We have to know that we can only spend the money which we have earned already. Additionally, we should not be deceived by advertisements which make needs out of wants! This is the only way to repair the broken foundation of our economy.

Time limit of debts

> At the end of every seven years you shall grant a release. And this is the manner of the release: every creditor shall release what he has lent to his neighbour. He shall not exact it of his neighbour, his brother, because the LORD's release has been proclaimed. Of a foreigner you may exact it, but whatever of yours is with your brother your hand shall release. (Deut. 15:1-3)

God has set a time limit to credits! He does not want people to be in bondage forever, because somebody who owes money is a kind of slave to the lender! While a stranger still has to pay the owed money, a brother or neighbor is released after seven years.

Is God biased against strangers? If you read in context, you will understand that it is not so. In the whole Bible, God is very concerned about protecting foreigners. They are more vulnerable because they don't have their own land. But in this case of lending, a foreigner is a higher risk. He might run away because he doesn't own any land anyway! There has to be a clear agreement on how he will pay back while he is not part of the sabbatical years of the Israelites. The problem, however, is that there is no accountability and no close relationship between a lender and a stranger. You don't know him well and you have no idea how he came into the situation he is in. Maybe it was because of mismanagement. That's why a foreigner has to pay back, so that he will learn how to use money well.

To the brothers and neighbors, however, the debt has to be released in the seventh year so that they have a fair chance to start new. God doesn't want people to get deeper and deeper into the debt trap. This rule also limits the amount which is to be lent. A lender should only lend a reasonable amount that can be paid back within the agreed time. Another advantage is that the debt will not pass on to the next generation, so the children don't have to pay for the parent's mistakes.

As it is a brother, he will be forgiven if he doesn't manage to pay back the whole amount within the agreed time. The disadvantage however, is that he cannot lend from the same person again. This principle teaches people to be honest so they have the possibility of getting further credit in the future.

From this scripture, we also learn that God set different levels of responsibility. Everyone is first responsible for his own family (children and parents), then for other relatives (brothers), thirdly for neighbors (village community), and finally for strangers.

Chapter 9

Ethics in Alternative Economy

Economy cannot work without ethics. They are the center of economics. What are ethics? Ethics is a branch of philosophy that addresses questions about morality – that is, concepts such as good and evil, right and wrong, virtue and vice, justice and injustice, etc. It deals with the values people apply in their life, for example, honesty, truthfulness and keeping of promises. Without these, there can be no economic progress. For the household to produce goods and services, it depends on good ethics. How can a farmer, for example, grow fruits if he is not sure whether he will eat the fruit of his labor? He will make sure first, that there are good laws that will protect his work and also that he will not be cheated in his sales through unjust trade policies. Without this, there will be decrease in the production of goods and services.

If people apply good ethics in their life, they produce an environment of trust in which businesses can flourish. This leads to a strong economy and wealth for the whole community. In the following we are going to look at ethical aspects which are very important for a successful economy.

Respecting private property

And you shall not steal.
(Deut. 5:19)

Stealing is very destructive for the economy. It has negative effects on the owner as well as on the thief. The owner stealing is an economic damage. He gets frustrated, angry and discouraged. He might have had an intention or a plan with the stolen money or property which is now frustrated through the stealing. So his loss is even bigger than the value of the stolen thing!

The thief might have a temporary economic advantage, although he can never sell the stolen thing to the value that it is worth. This might tempt him to steal again, which brings him in danger of wrong habits and of coming into conflict with the law, which can put him in prison. Once in prison, his whole family experiences an economic loss – the breadwinner has to be fed in prison now! This can bring his whole family into poverty.

Long term effect of stealing on economy

The effects described above are only the immediate ones. But the habit of stealing leads to an even bigger loss for the owners. Because of thieves, there is a need for security arrangements like grills, walls, locks and guards, which all cost money. As neither the thief nor the owner has an advantage from stealing, it is economic nonsense.

Widespread stealing even discourages people from planting, investing and producing (it will be stolen anyway and I will not enjoy the fruit of my work!). Once people think this way, production will be reduced communitywide, which results in lack of products and people being in poverty.

This is not the will of God for us! That's why he disallows stealing. He wants us to receive the fruit of our labor so that we enjoy our work, knowing that it's worth it. This way, production is increased and everyone has enough and has it in abundance. Through this command, God protects ownership; we have the right to private property!

When we think of stealing, we might have a picture of somebody going to a shop and taking things without paying. But there are many different ways of stealing. Some of the things which we might not think of, but are special and common ways of stealing are the following:

Tab. 3: Different ways of stealing

Way of stealing	Why is it stealing?
Personal debt	Stealing from your own future & from your children
National debt	Stealing from future generations
Burning fields & forest	Stealing from yourself & your neighbors (productivity of land decreases as soil loses fertility)
Bad stewardship of land (through pollution by plastic bags and other non-biodegradable waste)	Stealing from future generations: they have to invest more money to make the land usable and fertile again
Withholding wages of a laborer (Deut. 24:14-15)	Stealing from laborer (food, loss of health & capital, loss of profit as he could have invested money)

Arriving too late to an appointment, not keeping time	Stealing the time of others (they could have done something profitable in this time)

Thankfulness

And let the peace of Christ rule in your hearts, to which indeed you were called in one body. And be thankful.
(Col. 3:15)

As we mentioned already in the worldview chapter, jealousy is very destructive for an economy. That's why the tenth commandment is as follows:

> And you shall not covet your neighbour's wife. And you shall not desire your neighbour's house, his field, or his male servant, or his female servant, his ox, or his donkey, or anything that is your neighbour's. (Deut. 5:21)

Although coveting starts in the mind, it is a sin. Why is that so? It opens the door to many other sins. It causes people to misuse funds, to use wrong means of getting money (including stealing), to ask for bribes, to use witchcraft, which leads to conflicts in relationships.

Is there no positive side to coveting? Yes, there is. If you see the house of your neighbor and it motivates you to work harder so that you can build a house like his, it is positive. Whenever you desire a good thing and take the effort, work or time to obtain it, there is no problem with it. You may tell yourself: *"If he was able to learn this, I also am able to make the same effort and learn it"* or *"If she managed to save up enough for this, then I can save as well"*.

The problem of the destructive kind of coveting is that my eyes are on the things which I don't have. My thinking always goes in the same circle: *"if only I were ... then I would ...", "if only I had ... then I could ... "*. It focuses my eyes on what I am not, on what I don't have and what I can't do. It fills my mind with unrealities and impossibilities, which lead to discontentment and complaining, resentment and bitterness. This paralyzes my actions, makes me lazy and closes down my mind.

The opposite of jealousy is thankfulness. The Bible commands us to be thankful countless times. What does thankfulness do to my mind? Where are my eyes? What do I focus on? Thankfulness focuses my eyes on what I am, what I do or received and what is possible. It makes me aware of realities and possibilities. It opens doors and options for me. It makes me realize my potential. It helps us to be successful in economics because we can say, *"I may not have much, but I do have and with it I can do something!!"* Thankfulness even helps me to be faithful (remember that faithfulness is a strong requirement for a good economy). When I am thankful my attitude will always be, *"I will work with what I have."* God does not command us to be thankful because he is selfish, but because it is appropriate for him and good for our mental health.

Many people get sick today, more especially in Western Europe and the United States, because they are not thankful. The sickness caused by unthankfulness is called depression. At least that is one cause. You will also discover that more people will enjoy your company when you are thankful! It is your own choice, you can choose to be content or to be discontent and you will reap the fruit of it.

Honesty

The third important ethic to be successful in business is to be honest. We have to be honest in every area of our life. The Bible commands us again and again not to cheat others. Here are two sample scriptures:

> You shall not have in your bag two kinds of weights, a large and a small. You shall not have in your house two kinds of measures, a large and a small. A full and fair weight you shall have, a full and fair measure you shall have, that your days may be long in the land that the LORD your God is giving you. For all who do such things, all who behave dishonestly, are an abomination to the LORD your God. (Deut. 25:13-16)

> Unequal weights are an abomination (extremely unpleasant or unacceptable) to the LORD, and false scales are not good. (Prov. 20:23)

God commands honesty in trade. What is said must be done whether it is the agreed measure, quality, price or time. We are not to cheat! From the following chart we can learn the advantages of being honest in our business and the disadvantages if we cheat:

Tab.4: Consequences of Honesty and Cheating

Honesty: advantages	Cheating: disadvantages
... *so that you may live long in the land* ...	... *all who do such things, all who act dishonestly are an abomination to the LORD your God.*
Customers trust you: long-term relationships	Customer is frustrated, angry and discouraged to buy from you again.
Efficiency in trade concerning cost, time and	Customer is robbed of time, resources and
Word is honored: big amounts of materials can be traded quickly and cost-efficiently.	Breaking of word: Not reliable, complicated, and inefficient.
Increased creativity and investment leads to higher development.	Hurts the weak, poor and uneducated: profits the strong, rich and educated, makes the rich-poor divide wider, hinders and discourages the development of people, is against development
	The same as stealing: little gain for few people for a short time while a lot of loss for most people for a long time. This is economic nonsense.

Balance of work and rest

God commanded us to work as well as to rest. Both work and rest
are something good. But if we don't balance them well, it becomes a problem. Too much work is bad and too much rest is bad as well. Let's discuss what the bible teaches concerning these two:

Work

> *The LORD God took the man and put him in the Garden of Eden to work it and keep it. (Gen. 2:15)*

God commanded humans to work before sin ever happened. It is part of the perfect creation and not a punishment for sin. Work is good for humans. Somebody who does not work easily gets sick in mind and body.

There are two main misconceptions about work[4]:

Work as burden

Some people have the worldview that work is a burden. They think that it is something they have to do because their miserable body still binds
them to the physical world. In their understanding, work is not spiritual.The first thing they can think of, when their needs are covered is to stop working.

Work for money only

Others believe that work is valuable for producing the goods they want or the money to buy the pleasures they want.

---

[4] Three different work worldviews adapted from Darrow L. Miller, *Discipling Nations: The Power of Truth to Transform Cultures* (Seattle: YWAM Publishing, 2001), p. 248.

Whenever they work, their heart is only on the money they will get at the end of the month. What they live for is the time after work. It is the time they have for enjoyment by spending the money they earned.

These worldviews are totally missing the point. The Bible is teaching us a completely different attitude towards work:

Work as worship

Work is good and commanded by God. It's part of worship to God. It's something we should do wholeheartedly, something we can enjoy. The first purpose of work is to reveal God's character through the way we do it. Secondly, it's to serve others who are image bearers of God. Finally, it is to produce needed things and to provide for our living. We have to keep in mind that it glorifies God when we work and it gives us significance and satisfaction.

Both Jesus and God the Father are working. Jesus was a carpenter until he turned thirty years of age and even after that he said: "My Father is working until now, and I am working."[51] That's why Proverbs 10:4 exhorts us:

A slack hand causes poverty, but the hand of the diligent makes rich.

God demands us to work diligently. Laziness is not an option with God. Moreover, Hebrew language has only one word for work; whether a priest is doing his duty or a farmer ploughs his field. All work is equally important.

---

[51] John 5:17

Rest

God made a day for rest from the creation of the earth:

> Thus the heavens and the earth were finished, and all the host of them. And on the seventh day God finished his work that he had done, and he rested on the seventh day from all his work that he had done. So God blessed the seventh day and made it holy, because on it God rested from all his work that he had done in creation. (Gen. 2:1-3)

Why did God rest? Was he tired? Is there any weakness in him? The answer is no, "The LORD is the everlasting God, the Creator of the ends of the earth. He does not faint or grow weary"[52]. God stopped working to enjoy the work of his hands. He wants us to do the same!

Later, he reinforced the Sabbath in the Ten Commandments:

> Observe the Sabbath day, to keep it holy, as the LORD your God commanded you. Six days you shall labour and do all your work, but the seventh day is a Sabbath to the LORD your God. On it you shall not do any work, you or your son or your daughter or your male servant or your female servant, or your ox or your donkey or any of your livestock, or the sojourner who is within your gates, that your male servant and your female servant may rest as well as you. You shall remember that you were a slave in the land of Egypt, and the LORD your God brought you out from there with a mighty hand and an outstretched arm. Therefore the LORD your God commanded you to keep the Sabbath day. (Deut. 5:12-15)

Here God adds two more reasons for the Sabbath rest:

- A day of recreation (in contrast to the slavery in Egypt): A time to rest physically, mentally,

---

[52] Is. 40:28

emotionally and spiritually. It is for maintenance and restoration, not only for us, but also for our children, our workers and our animals.

- A time to connect with God and to have extended time for relationships: "The Sabbath was made for man, not man for the Sabbath"[53].

In summary, we learn from the Bible to work diligently for six days and to rest one day. On Sunday, we have time to connect with God, to reflect, evaluate and re-direct our work and to enjoy the work of God's (creation) and our hands.

Stewardship
As each has received a gift, use it to serve one another, as good stewards of God's varied grace. (1Pet. 4:10)

In the previous chapter about work, we read from Genesis that God told men to keep the Earth. And again in the scripture above from the New Testament, we read that we are called to be good stewards of the things God has given us. A steward is somebody who takes care of the things of his master. What he is dealing with is not his own and he does not have a right to destroy it. In the same way, we are stewards of the money, time, land, and resources which God has given us. Therefore, we have to be careful that we don't misuse them! We have to invest the money wisely and give freely to those in need, we have to make good use of our time, take care of the land, rivers, mountains, trees and animals which God has given to us. Sometimes we steal the money given into our care or the money of others by not doing things in time (see topic: stealing). Now we are going to look more closely at the stewardship of land.

---

[53] Mark 2:27

Stewardship of Land

God does not only give man a command to rest, but also a command for the land to rest. Land is the most important factor when we talk about economy. All products start from the land. Any type of business is dependent on land.

> When you come into the land that I give you, the land shall keep a Sabbath to the LORD. For six years you shall sow your field, and for six years you shall prune your vineyard and gather in its fruits, but in the seventh year there shall be a Sabbath of solemn rest for the land, a Sabbath to the LORD. You shall not sow your field or prune your vineyard. You shall not reap what grows of itself in your harvest, or gather the grapes of your undressed vine. It shall be a year of solemn rest for the land. (Lev. 25:2-5)

Through this scripture, God affirms our rights, but also our responsibilities to work the land. No matter what we do on the land, we have to maintain its fertility. Overuse has to be prevented. The time of rest regenerates the land and increases its fertility, which leads to higher productivity. That's why stewardship is so essential for a good economy and for successful agriculture in particular.

God was very serious about this command. The reason for the exile of the Israelites to Babylon was that people did not obey the command to rest the land:

He took into exile in Babylon those who had escaped from the sword, and they became servants to him and to his sons ... until the land had enjoyed its Sabbaths. All the days that it lay desolate it kept Sabbath, to fulfill seventy years. (2Chr. 36:20-21)

The length of the exile is determined by their missing Sabbaths for the land! God is serious about land and land fertility: Environmental protection is very much on God's heart!

Land ownership

> *The land shall not be sold in perpetuity, for the land is*
> *mine. For you are strangers and sojourners with me.*
> *(Lev. 25:23)*

From this scripture, we learn that we are not the only owner of our land! It had owners before you; it will have other owners after you (children, to whom it will be passed on). But you, as owners, are accountable to the owners after you: will the land still be usable and fertile after you have lived on it?

If you overuse or exploit the land, you are stealing from future owners. We don't have the right to do that! Moreover, God is the ultimate Owner of all land. He allots land for a time to people, but they are only 'aliens' or 'tenants'. While we have the right to use it, we don't have the right to harm or destroy it. Whatever we do with the land, we are answerable before God, the ultimate owner.

Things which increase fertility of the land and things which destroy it:

Tab.5: Habits which add fertility or destroy the land

Adds fertility	Destroys land
Putting compost on the land	Putting plastic bottles, jumbos and other waste which cannot turn into soil
Covering the ground with compostable things (protection from sun, increase of positive microorganisms)	Leaving the ground bare, burning the leftovers (destroying positive microorganisms which make the ground fertile)
Planting trees	Cutting trees without replacement
Use of natural fertilizer (manure, ...)	Use of chemical fertilizer
Crop rotation & Sabbath for land	Planting the same crop every year

Now we can easily understand why this ethical principle is so important for a strong economy: If the soil is fertile, it produces much fruit and brings prosperity. If we use the land anyway, we destroy the productivity of the land and become poor.

That's why it is very important to learn farming in God's way!

Chapter 10

Practical outworking of Economy: Having a business

In this chapter, we will first define the term business and who a business person is. Afterwards, we will discuss important things to consider when starting a business. Then, we will look at different types of businesses and their advantages and disadvantages. Finally, we will explain how to write a business plan and how to maintain a business (bookkeeping).

What is business? Business is the act of trading goods and services with the aim of making profit. This is the worldly understanding. But from the biblical point of view, it is the act of trading goods and services as acts of worship to God.

Who is a business person? A business person is someone who is actively involved in the trading of goods and services, and serves customers as an act of worship to God. His aim is not to make money, but profit comes as a by-product of good relationships with customers, suppliers and the service done to them.

How to start a business

If you plan to start a business, there are a number of things to think about and to consider. Here, we are just giving a few principles which will help you think through your plan of how to structure your business and how to implement it: Begin small, start with your own strength, increase little by little, don't allow people to destroy your business through credits, and reinvest your profit!

Small beginning, big future

And though your beginning was small, your latter days will be very great. (Job 8:7)

In the world today, many people want to start big, but in the world of God, we learn that even if our beginning is small, we will become great. The advantage of starting small is that it is easier to manage. As the business grows, you increase in knowledge and skills of business management. If we took someone who has never done business before and put him in the leading position of a bank would he manage it? Could he deal with these huge sums of money? The bank will definitely go down. What is the problem? This person has never handled this amount of money before. He does not know how to deal with it and how he can attract customers. If you want to be successful in your business, it is better to start small. If you start your small business and are faithful, you will end up big. But if you cannot manage a small business, how do you think you can manage a big one? Everything big once started small!

Start with your own strength

When you start a business, think about the things which you can do (see topic: thankfulness) and analyze your capital (see topic: capital & profit). Don't depend on borrowing money. The lending institutions want to profit from you! They give you a loan so that their money will work for them through you. Instead of working for yourself, you will be working for them:

> The rich rules over the poor and the borrower is the slave
> of the lender. (Prov. 22:7)

According to this scripture, you will be a slave to the lending institution.

The solution is to start with your own capital. As we discussed before, your capital is not the money but the properties and skills you have. If you want to have more capital, you can even partner with others who have other capital that you don't have. We will come back to partnership later.

The worst thing that can happen is being in continual debts because of borrowing money. This will take away the joy of working. Even your family will be in trouble if you cannot pay back the money. You will have to always work for the past. Credits usually come with high interest. Let's look at a scripture illustrating this:

> Now the wife of one of the sons of the prophets cried to
> Elisha, "Your servant my husband is dead, and you
> know that your servant feared the LORD, but the creditor
> has come to take my two children to be his slaves."(2
> Kings 4:1)

This scripture teaches us how serious borrowing can be. The borrower here was a godly man, a prophet, but yet he left his family in financial debts when he died. Then the creditors came to his wife and wanted to take her only source of joy, her two sons, away. If this prophet had started from his own strength and had failed in business, he would have left them neither wealth nor debt, which would have been better for them. That's why the Bible says:

> A good man leaves an inheritance to his children's children, but the sinner's wealth is laid up for the righteous. (Prov. 13:22)

If you do business with the principles described here, you will leave an inheritance for your children. This has to be your motivation! Your children should have a head start in their life and not inherit your trouble. Be as King David: Before he died, he prepared everything for his son Solomon, even the material to build the temple for God. That's why Solomon was even greater than David, because he had a good start in life. Just imagine if Solomon had to start with debts that his father left at his death!

Increase little by little

> *Wealth gained hastily will dwindle, but whoever gathers little by little will increase it. (Prov. 13:11)*
>
> *Do not toil to acquire wealth; be discerning enough to desist. When your eyes light on it, it is gone, for suddenly it sprouts wings, flying like an eagle toward heaven. (Prov. 23:4-5)*

An important principle in marketing is to build long term relationships with customers and suppliers. If you cheat them, you cannot have a good relationship with them and your business cannot survive without them. From the scriptures above, we learn that it is not wise to aim on quick profit. In your heart, you should aim to serve your customers by selling them your goods at a good price. A satisfied customer will tell their friends and they too will come, and so, your market will increase by word of mouth. In this way, you will increase more and more, in customers and sales, and your business will grow slowly, but steadily. Because your customers increase, you will sell more over a long time. If you aim, however, to double your price to gain profit quickly, you will lose your customers. That's what every non-Christian does. But a Christian must have the vision of a business with biblical principles: respecting and serving the customer and not the profit first. Your profit will be the fruit of your faithfulness to God by serving the customers who are made in God's image!

Don't allow credits

You shall give him his wages on the same day, before the sun sets (for he is poor and counts on it), lest he cry against you to the LORD, and you be guilty of sin.
(Deut. 24:15)

The scripture above teaches us not to withhold the wages of a laborer. Whenever you employ someone, and agree to pay him the same day or at the end of the month, you need to keep your word! The same way, you should not allow your customers to buy things from your business on credit. They have to pay the same day they get the goods, because you depend on this money for the expansion or even the continuation of your newly started business. One of the biggest mistakes is starting a new business and allowing customers to take your goods on credit. It is more dangerous in the beginning because you don't have a big capital yet, including little experience in how to manage it. If your customers tell you that they will pay the money next week and the following week they cannot pay, you are in trouble because you cannot buy new goods due to the lack of money. That's why it is advisable to start with a business in which people can pay on a cash basis only.

Reinvest your profit

And the rain fell, and the floods came, and the winds blew and beat on that house, but it did not fall, because it had been founded on the rock. (Matt. 7:25)

When you start your business, you should already have a plan on how you want your business to increase. As we mentioned in the beginning of this chapter, it is good to start small. Building up on the bird's nest principle, (see chapter 8) let's assume somebody starts with one chicken that lays eggs. Now, he could take all the eggs and eat or sell them. In this way, he will have a constant business with always the same amount of profit. If he wants to increase, however, he will leave some of the eggs with the chicken so that it can hatch them. Now, the business will increase through an increase in chickens, which will soon start producing eggs as well. If you have five chickens, each producing eggs, and you leave every chicken with two eggs to hatch again, soon you will have fifteen chickens. What do we learn from this example? It is better to reinvest profit than to eat it all. By reinvesting, the business grows quickly and starts producing more profit and therefore, higher income.

Once you gather a bigger amount of profit, it will even be better to start investing in something other than chickens, because a wise man does not put all his eggs in one basket! A sickness might come and kill all your chickens, but if you are wise, you would buy real estate with your profit, for example a piece of land. Even if all your chickens die, you will still have the land which is a safer capital and will help you to stand up again if your business fails. This is like building on the rock in the scripture above. The importance of investing in real estate is that it does not lose its value. This means you will not lose everything if a financial crisis comes, because your land will remain your land. Even if you make a mistake in your business, you can recover easily when you have a piece of land or even a house.

In conclusion, our advice is, don't eat all your profit and don't put it into the bank either! As we discussed earlier in chapter eight, money does not have value in itself; it's just a currency. If inflation comes, it will all be lost!

How to maintain a business
Commit your work to the LORD, and your plans will be established. (Prov. 16:3)

After starting a business, our main goal is to keep the business running and growing well. We cannot have a successful business if we don't include God from the beginning. Even non-believers dedicate their business to what they believe. As we want to glorify God through our work, we need to pray in every stage of our business to get God's instructions and His wisdom. To glorify God, your business also needs to be a blessing to the disadvantaged. Coming back to the scripture above, we see that there are two steps we need to take to be successful. We need to commit our work to the Lord (praying and listening) and then our plans will be established. This suggests that we have a plan already. We don't just pray and wait without making plans. In order to plan well, we have to know something about business cycle management. There are four stages in the business which are in a continuous circle. That's why it is called "cycle management".

The first stage is the identification of the market. You have to do some investigation about opportunities and challenges. The goal is to find something needed at your place which is not yet provided. In this process, you calculate what the challenges and threats of this business might be. To do this investigation, you have to go to the place where you want to start your business and do a survey there.

Based on this survey, you make a plan. This is the second stage. You plan what your service will be and how you can make sure that your business will continue in terms of finances, availability of commodities, customer care and so on. Think about how to encourage customers to come to you and how you can market your product. You need good marketing strategies so that your business can survive in the beginning, when you are not yet well known in the place. Maybe you can offer your products cheaper or with better quality or better services than your competitors.

The third stage is now the implementation of the plan. This is the actual starting point of the business. In this phase, you need to be careful in reviewing and monitoring the progress. Take care of your goods, so they will not be stolen by thieves. And if it is a good business, people will copy your idea and start doing the same. How will you cope with such a situation? Are you prepared to be better than them?

The fourth stage is called evaluation. This is important, because it helps you to do predictions for the future of your business. You have to evaluate whether you are fulfilling your actual plan, and if not, see what needs to be adjusted. Calculate everything and see whether the business is coming up to the actual plan. In context of biblical economy, you have to ask the question, whether the business' first goal is really serving customers. Or have you been taken up by the profit you are making, so that you forget that your first purpose is to serve God. If you don't follow those ethics, your business will inevitably start to break, because you don't really take care of your customers. If you have a partnership, you have to sit down with your partners to discuss what can be done. Don't just do something without the consent of your partner, this might weaken your relationship and become a threat to your business.

After the evaluation, you might have identified some challenges and new opportunities. A new cycle with identification of the market, a new design and implementation, might help you to adjust your business in a way that it can continue to grow. As we discussed already, when you grow little by little, you learn in every stage and every cycle, which will help you to improve your business as it grows.

Types of businesses

> Two are better than one, because they have a good reward for their toil. For if they fall one will lift up his fellow. But woe to him who is alone when he falls and has not another to lift him up! Again, if two lie together, they keep warm, but how can one keep warm alone? And though a man might prevail against one who is alone, two will withstand him--a threefold cord is not quickly broken. (Eccl. 4:9-12)

There are different types of business, for example sole trade and partnership businesses. A sole trader is somebody who manages his business alone. This has advantages as well as disadvantages:

Tab.6: Advantages and Disadvantages of Sole Trade Business

Advantages	Disadvantages
Flexibility: change of business possible	Limited in scope and capacity
All profit for one person	Loss has to be carried by a single person
You are your own boss (decide by yourself)	Limited creativity (no input of ideas from another person)
	Sickness destroys the business: nobody to work during the time of sickness

A partnership business is an enterprise run by more than one person. They share responsibilities, agree on how to run the business and carry the risks and profits of the business together. The advantages and disadvantages are the following:

Tab.7: Advantages and Disadvantages of Partnership Business

Advantages	Disadvantages
High creativity (input of ideas from several people)	Disagreement among partners blocks the business.
High scope and capacity (higher capital, higher mortgage/credit from bank, greater territory of influence, better buying conditions due to bigger amounts)	If partners don't have the same vision and same worldview, it does not work!
Risks are shared (shared risk is half risk! Sickness cannot destroy the business because the partner will carry on, a loss will be divided among the parties, etc.)	Profit is shared among the partners.
High accountability (limits possibility of immoral behavior, less mismanagement)	Business is not flexible (no quick decisions possible)

We have seen that both kinds of businesses have advantages as well as disadvantages. But, we learn from the Bible that a partnership business has more advantages than a sole trade business (see scriptures above). Solomon, the wisest man in the Old Testament, knew that there is much evil under the sun[54]. His conclusion of this matter is that two are better than one. Two together can better withstand adversity. Whether a thief is coming to steal or somebody wants to cheat you in a bigger decision or when one falls sick – the partnership business is better. Solomon also addresses the problem of envy among neighbors, which causes them both more toil while they cannot enjoy the fruit of it[55]. Solomon

---

[54] Eccl.4:1

says that this is not leading anywhere, but people have to help each other and partner together in their work. Three are even better than two, for a threefold cord is not quickly broken[56].

Even when we go back to the very root of our existence, the creation of man in Genesis 1, we discover that we were meant to live in relationship or partnership with others.

> Then God said, "Let us make man in our image, after our likeness. And let them have dominion over the fish of the sea and over the birds of the heavens and over the livestock and over all the earth and over every creeping thing that creeps on the earth." So God created man in his own image, in the image of God he created him; male and female he created them. (Gen. 1:26-27)

God, named 'elohim' in this passage, means a compound unity. It is plural and at the same time used as singular in the grammatical structure. Our God is a God who is not alone. That's why he says "let *us* make man". It is the three in one God, the Father, Son and Holy Spirit. They live in unity, but enjoy the diversity of each person of the trinity. As we were created in the image of God, we are to be the same in relationship with others. It is written "in the image of God he created **them**". It is not Adam that was in the image of God, but Adam and Eve together. We can only have dominion on Earth when we live the way God intended us to live: in partnership. That's why a business run by partners will be more successful than one run by a sole trader. Because our God is three in one, there is a relationship, accountability, creativity and submission in Him. All these are the properties which a

---

55 Eccl. 4:4
56 Eccl. 4:12

successful partnership business needs. We can learn a lot from God!

Business plan

The plans of the diligent lead surely to abundance, but everyone who is hasty comes only to poverty.
(Prov. 21:5)

A business plan describes a business idea with the arrangements to fulfill the plan. Normally, it's used to convince capital givers, like a bank or a private investor, about a good business idea and to receive credit as starting capital from them. That's the world's approach concerning business plans. In the Bible, however, we learn that it is important to make a good plan first to have a successful business. Not having a good plan leads to poverty! This means we have to analyze what capital we have and make a wise plan on how to increase it. This also means that we don't just focus on getting credit, but on what we have and what we can do with it. To start a business with lasting value, it is important to answer the following five questions:

1. What's the idea of the business?

Describe in detail what kind of business you want to have in a way that somebody who doesn't know you and your area of expertise can understand.

2. Values

Explain your values and principles and how you plan to implement them. This should show how you want to glorify God with your business.

3. How will you fulfill your plans?

Describe the steps you are going to take and include the following information:

- Financial plan for the first year (s. Budgeting)
- Description of the starting capital and how it will be used
- Description of the estimated profit
- What will be done with the profit? How much will be re-invested into the business?

Example: If you start with a field and 5000 kwacha; what will you do with these two things? What do you expect your profits will be in a month?

4. What will the business look like in 1 year?

Describe the level of business you wish to have in one year. How big will your business be? How many workers will you have? How much capital will you have accumulated? What will your profit be? How will you develop your business (ideas of expansion or change of business)?

5. What will it look like after one year? (future perspective, long-term goal)

What dreams do you have for your business?

Suggestions for starting: Build a team of 3 to 4 people and discuss the different kinds of capital you have, as we showed already that partnership business has more advantages. After analyzing all the capital you have, then come up with a business idea, which you can start by using the capital you have. After agreeing on the business idea, answer the five questions above. Make sure that you treat question number three in detail giving a well-structured plan concerning the first year of your new business, which will be a foundation for a successful start.

Budgeting
For which of you, desiring to build a tower, does not first sit down and count the cost, whether he has enough to complete it? (Luk. 14:28)

The first step to financial success is to count the costs. Financial planning or budgeting has three main goals:

1. Control: It controls your day-to-day finances to enable you to increase your capacity in life and your business.
2. Reaching goals: It helps to choose and follow a course toward long-term financial goals such as getting real estate (e.g. house or land).
3. Protection: It helps to build a financial safety net to prevent financial disasters caused by catastrophes like famine, earthquake, illness and so on (s. natural evil).

Therefore, budgeting is equally useful for a little business, a big company or even your family. Budgeting means planning your finances. It is a plan for your future earnings and expenditures. You will already have a record of some of the data, but other data you will need to predict. Making a budget helps you to have an overview of your whole business and will increase your income and profit. In practice, budgeting means writing a list with all your upcoming income and expenditures.

Imagine that you get a fixed salary of two thousand dollars next month. Then, you try to make a plan for your family. How much does each child receive? Do we have enough money to buy a new bike? Do we have enough money to buy Coke or other drinks instead of making tea? Is it possible to save some money for the school fees which we have to pay in 3 months? To answer all these questions, we have to look at our spending priorities. For example, what is the most important and what is the least important:

1. Commitments / Obligation: Fixed amounts which you really have to pay. You already know in advance, that you have to pay this amount. Some examples are:

- House rent/bills

- school fees for children

2. Need: You can influence the amount of money you will spend in this category. Examples:

- Food: You need a certain amount of food to survive, but you can influence how much money you want to spent for food. You can plant your own vegetables and fruit in your garden. This approach will be cheaper than buying food in the big supermarket. If you buy imported food, it's much more expensive than buying products produced in your own country.

- Clothes: You can buy new fashions every time, which will be more expensive than buying just the clothes you need. The clothes we need cover our nakedness – they are not mainly for fashion! Of course we need to dress nice, but it is important to keep the balance and not just to start the habit of buying more and more, while you have appropriate clothes in your wardrobe at home.

3. Want: Luxury products; it's not absolutely necessary. Example:

- New car: it's not necessary if your old car is still working.

4. Saving: After a period of time (month, year) it's important to save some money for future expenditures. You can bring this money to the bank or you can treasure it at home. But make sure that you don't use the money this month, because it's for a difficult situation in the future (safety net). For example, the harvest might not be as good as expected next month. For this reason, you will have a lower profit. To fill this lack of profit, you can use the money you saved last month. You can also put money aside to buy something expensive, for example, a bike.

After writing down the "commitment" and "needs" you can calculate how much money is left for the "wants". Every month, it is good to put something into your bank account. This will increase your savings. It's important to divide up your money in this way. If you spend the money the way you want and you always buy whatever you see, you are in danger of not having enough money for the "commitment". Maybe you will have a new car, but not enough to eat.

The four categories mentioned above are subdivisions of your income. If you add them up, you will have the whole income. If you increase the expenditures of "wants", logically it means that you will have less money for the "needs" and "savings".

Financial plan

In addition to the system of budgeting mentioned above, in a business, a financial plan has to be made. This serves to plan the use of the profit which must cover the salaries of the workers and reinvestment.

It is important to save a certain amount of the profit to cover unforeseen events such as a natural catastrophe. This might around 5% from the revenues and will help in restarting the business in an event of disaster. It can be used to buy real estate, which is a safe place to keep the money.

Another part of the profit should be reinvested in the business so that it can grow. Coming back to the bird's nest principle, it means not eating all eggs or chicks, but raising some chicks to become fully grown chicken, which will also lay eggs. Try to think long term. See the advantages you have in the future and try to plan ahead to the future months and years.

Bookkeeping: Cash book

A cash book is a book or piece of paper where all transactions that lead to an out payment or an incoming payment are recorded. The following information is given by a cash book:

- number of receipt
- date
- account
- text
- revenues / income
- expenses
- net total (difference between revenues and expenditures)

With a cash book, you have an overview of your expenditures and revenues during a certain period of time. For example, in the evening you can look at how much money you earned.

Conclusion

After reading this book on poverty and alternative economy, it is important to remember that it is God who gives us the ability to create wealth. You may think that after reading the advice of this book, everything will work out well for you, but this is not a magic book! If you do not have a personal relationship with the God of the Bible who created all these principles, it will be difficult for you to effectively apply these ideas in the long term and prosper and build a strong economy. As we discussed earlier, broken relationships are the root cause of poverty. We first have to know how these relationships can be restored. This is not just an economic issue; it includes humanity as a whole. If people want to live fulfilled lives – a state where they are neither materially nor socially nor psychologically nor spiritually poor - they need a personal relationship with Jesus Christ. By accepting Him as personal Lord and Savior who gave His life for the world to restore all broken relationships, our relationships can be healed. The principles themselves, however, are universal and work for you, even if you worship another god. But they will not help you to overcome the four levels of evils described in this book. It all starts with the transformation of you!

The goal of this book, however, is not just to help you, but is to transform whole communities and nations. If you are the only one applying these principles, it will be very hard or even impossible to prosper. That's why you need to get people around you, who will agree to the same ethics and principles, the same worldview and therefore, the same God. Then, these people, under God's leading, should seek to bring Godly influence into the places of authority, so that the different areas of society (for example, the economy) reflect the principles of the Bible and ultimately, the character of the one true God.

There is a scripture in Ecclesiastics which summarizes all that has been discussed in this book:

> Now all has been heard, here is the conclusion of the matter: Fear God and keep his commandment, for this is the whole duty of man. (Eccl. 12:13)

References

- Ashimolowo, M. (2007). *What is wrong with Being Black?* Shippensburg: Destiny Image Publishers
- British Prime Minister Margarat Thatcher, 1988, quotet in Mangalwadi, (2011). *The Book that made your world*, p.161 et seq.)
- Cambridge Learners Dictionnary (2005). Cambridge: Cambridge University Press.
- Cunningham. L., (2007). *The Book that Transforms Nations: The power of the Bible to change any country.* Seattle: YWAM Publishing
- Kirk, R (1991). *The Roots of American Order.* Washington, DC: Regenery Gateway, p. 29.
- Mankiw & Taylor(2006). Economics, p. 27.
- Pritzl, K. (2010). *Truth: studies of a robust presence.* The Catholic University of America Press, p. 127-131
- Weikart, R. (2004). *From Darwin to Hitler.* Hampshire: PALGRAVE MACMILLAN

www.ingramcontent.com/pod-product-compliance
Lightning Source LLC
Chambersburg PA
CBHW060618210326
41520CB00010B/1382